CW00348865

FOOD

FABIO PARASECOLI

The MIT Press | Cambridge, Massachusetts | London, England

This book was set in Chaparral Pro by Toppan Best-set Premedia Limited.
Printed and bound in the United States of America.

Library of Congress Cataloging-in-Publication Data

Names: Parasecoli, Fabio, author.
Title: Food / Fabio Parasecoli.
Description: Cambridge, MA : The MIT Press, 2019. | Series: The MIT Press
  essential knowledge series | Includes bibliographical references and index.
Identifiers: LCCN 2018048623 | ISBN 9780262537315 (pbk. : alk. paper)
Subjects: LCSH: Food. | Nutrition. | Food supply. | Food security.
Classification: LCC TX353 .P355 2019 | DDC 641.3—dc23
LC record available at https://lccn.loc.gov/2018048623

10   9   8   7   6   5   4   3   2   1

CONTENTS

SERIES FOREWORD

The MIT Press Essential Knowledge series offers accessible, concise, beautifully produced pocket-size books on topics of current interest. Written by leading thinkers, the books in this series deliver expert overviews of subjects that range from the cultural and the historical to the scientific and the technical.

In today's era of instant information gratification, we have ready access to opinions, rationalizations, and superficial descriptions. Much harder to come by is the foundational knowledge that informs a principled understanding of the world. Essential Knowledge books fill that need. Synthesizing specialized subject matter for nonspecialists and engaging critical topics through fundamentals, each of these compact volumes offers readers a point of access to complex ideas.

Bruce Tidor
Professor of Biological Engineering and Computer Science
Massachusetts Institute of Technology

Everybody eats. Inevitably, we think we are experts—and, in a way, we are. How does one start to write a book about food? We all experience food in different ways, and we tend to have strong feelings and ideas about it. Moreover, many consumers around the world share a growing feeling that something is wrong with what and how we eat. What can be done to improve such a ubiquitous aspect of everyday life?

The book you're reading is inevitably idiosyncratic, marked by my personal history, my interests, and my experiences as a journalist in foreign politics, as a food critic, and lately as a food studies scholar. My challenge has been to take an immense amount of information—often very complicated and requiring knowledge in fields ranging from economics to politics, from agriculture to technology—and make it accessible and even enjoyable. Embracing the approach of MIT's Essential Knowledge series, I've opted for a footnote-light style without renouncing accuracy of information and without shying away from complicated arguments.

Born and raised in Italy, educated in Italy, China, and Germany, a world traveler for work and fun, and now a professor in New York City, one of the most interesting and inclusive (but also parochial) cities on Earth, I tried to keep the perspective of this book as global as possible. I offer cases and examples from all around the world and embrace the point of view of a "we" located in the Global North but remain open and sensitive to other ways of life and to different realities. By *Global North*, a term that I'll be using through the book, I refer to the most economically developed countries and regions located in the Northern Hemisphere, such as Canada, the United States, Western Europe, and Japan, as well as Australia and New Zealand in the Southern Hemisphere. By exclusion, the *Global South* denotes instead a very diverse array of countries, ranging from political superpowers, such as China and India, to other nations in Central and South America, Africa, the Middle East, South Asia, and Southeast Asia. These are broad generalizations, which are unfortunately inevitable in a small book that deals with huge issues, but they nevertheless reflect the fundamental dynamics and divides that dominate the global economy, especially from the point of view of food production, distribution, and consumption.

I focus on topics that allow readers to understand their involvement in the complex and worldwide networks of *food systems*: from the familiar and the nearby to the foreign and the faraway. As climate change and political tensions have become global issues, affecting what and how we eat, we cannot pretend that what happens in remote locations and communities does not affect us, one way or another. I chose not to delve deeply into aspects of food such as its relevance in terms of cultural and social identity, its role in defining communities at all levels, its use as a political symbol, and its growing presence in the media, among others. These are all important phenomena that deserve attention and analysis, but they lie outside the scope of this book, which focuses instead on the functioning of food systems, their shortcomings, and what can be done to improve them.

My goal is to remind consumers that they are also citizens: their choices and purchases are not the only tools they have to influence what is produced and what reaches their tables. Many issues are much too complex and far-reaching to be affected only by personal decisions, made in the hope that markets respond to economic signals on the demand side. Real change requires coordinated efforts that involve stakeholders as diverse as individuals and communities of consumers and producers, activists, distributors, marketers, retailers, chefs, scientists and nutritionists, designers and engineers, financial institutions, transnational corporations, local and national authorities, and international organizations, just to mention a few. Voting with our wallets isn't enough: forms of collective and political action are necessary and urgent. I hope this book offers some tools to navigate the intricacies of the global food system, empowering readers to further their understanding of the factors that influence—and in some cases shape—their food choices. I believe that awareness is a powerful weapon.

Voting with our wallets isn't enough: forms of collective and political action are necessary and urgent. ... I believe that awareness is a powerful weapon.

ACKNOWLEDGMENTS

I want to start my acknowledgments by expressing the deepest appreciation for my family and friends, as their love through highs and lows and recent sorrows has never deserted me.

A special thank you to Doran Ricks for his support and encouragement during the writing process, as well as his company during well-deserved breaks.

I am indebted to Marion Nestle (New York University [NYU]), Sakiko Fukuda-Parr (The New School), and Nevin Cohen (City University of New York [CUNY]) for providing expert feedback on portions of the manuscript.

My gratitude goes to Mateusz Halawa, who read the manuscript through the eyes of the curious, smart, educated, but not necessarily expert reader that I tried to write for. His comments have been crucial to make the book clearer and more accessible.

I also want to thank my colleagues at NYU, The New School, the University of Gastronomic Sciences, and the Bologna Business School with whom I have often discussed the topics included in this book: Bea Banu, Christopher London, Ana Batista, Thomas Forster, Andy Smith, Kristin Reynolds, Joel Towers, Jonsara Ruth, Brian McGrath, Adam Brent, Carolin Mees, Rositsa Ilieva, Carolyn Dimitri, Mireya Loza, Krishnendu Ray, Jennifer Berg, Amy Bentley,

Beth Weitzman, Domingo Piñero, Lisa Sasson, Sonali McDermid, Stefani Bardin, Franco Fassio, Andrea Pieroni, Nicola Perullo, Simone Cinotto, Max Bergami, and Ludovica Leone.

I am grateful to the generous people who inspired me to think differently about design, objects, technology, and systems: in no precise order, Sonia Massari, Sonja Stummerer, Martin Hablesreiter, Marije Vogelzang, Katja Gruijters, Francesca Zampollo, Rick Schifferstein, Albert Fuster Martí, Mariana Eidler Díaz, Ricardo Bonacho, Pedro Reissig, Stefano Maffei, Antonello Fusetti, Catherine Flood, May Rosenthal Sloan, Andrés Sicard Currea, Freddy Zapata, Juan José Arango Correa, Noel Gonzalez, Malena Pasin, Daniel Bergara, Diego Labarca, Damián Valles, Victoria Molina, Mónica Silva, Aya Al Kadhimi, Janson Cheng, and Noah Allison.

Some chefs have motivated me to reflect on food systems, each in their own unique way: Dan Barber, Massimo Bottura, Alex Atala, Rene Redzepi, Jehangir Mehta, Pierre Thiam, Michael Elégbèdé, and Roberto Flore.

This book has been partly made possible thanks to the startup fund provided to me by New York University, Steinhardt School of Culture, Education, and Human Development and by grant DEC-2017/27/B/HS2/01338 provided by the National Science Centre, Poland.

FOOD: A CITIZEN'S MANUAL

Let's pause for a second ... We are all busy with work, family, friends, and fun activities, but whatever we do, the need to eat, relatively regularly, with more or less interest or gusto, is inevitable. If we live in a fairly developed country and our income allows us to make comfortable choices regarding what to consume, endless possibilities lie in front of us. However, in light of economic and social constraints, we may struggle to get enough nutritious and healthy food on a daily basis. In fact, many factors influence our decisions: financial circumstances, social status, ethical concerns, or simply a desire for a pleasurable eating experience. On any given day, we could decide to go to a supermarket that provides year-round access to fresh fruit and vegetables, as well as packaged products from all over the world. If the budget is a bit tight, we can opt to go to a big-box or discount store; discounts, buy two, get one free offers, and coupons to save some money are everywhere. If we so choose (and our finances allow for it), we can instead enjoy a stroll at a farmers' market and buy fresh, organic produce, possibly from the persons who grew it. Those of us who prefer a more hands-on approach can join a community garden and grow our own food, even in the middle of a city; we can decide to drive out to the countryside and purchase food directly from producers or become members of a *community-supported agriculture* (CSA) initiative.

In a splurging mood, we could visit a gourmet store and indulge in a slice of our favorite imported cheese: more expensive than your run-of-the-mill dairy, but oh, so good! And it comes with a story: real people made it, in a specific place that is different from any other place, with its own landscape, history, and traditions. While working with the cooperative Junta Local in Rio de Janeiro in its bimonthly market, I found myself selling roasted sweet potatoes and learned so much—not only about the producers and the products, but also about the consumers who came to enjoy the relatively cheap treat. If we get out of work late and we don't feel like shopping or cooking, we can have dinner at a restaurant, choosing from establishments that include fine dining, local farm-to-table eateries, hipster cafes, diners, or mom-and-pop holes-in-the-wall, depending on the spur-of-the-moment choice, our budget, and our location. We can choose comfort staples, ethnic cuisines, or just what we grew up eating as children; of course, each of us has experienced a different upbringing, with different availability and accessibility of food, geographical provenance, exposure to different culinary traditions, and various degrees of—or absence of—privilege.

A takeaway shop or a fast food joint is usually at hand, and it's convenient to order over the phone for delivery. Actually, if we don't want to talk to anybody, we could use an app to place our order, even adding the tip to the credit card payment so that all interactions with other human beings are avoided—and at times, we all feel like that. If we're in a cooking mood instead, we can flip through our favorite cookbooks, go online and browse for recipes, or just prepare those surefire dishes that we may have learned from family members, friends, or our favorite TV chefs. And if deciding what to eat and shopping for ingredients is too stressful, we can order a meal kit, with all the necessary ingredients neatly packaged, refrigerated, and delivered to our door.

Choices Are Complicated

Of course, all these opportunities are available to us if we reside in a location where a variety of services exist and so long as we have money to pay for it (or we have good credit). As citizens of modern, developed, and more or less affluent postindustrial democratic societies (frequently referred to as the Global North), when it comes to shopping, we have so many choices that buying what we want when we want it at affordable prices is almost experienced as a right. These opportunities are increasingly available—although still limited in number and variety—to middle-class, educated dwellers of large metropolises in the Global South, such as Bangkok, Accra, or Bogotá.[1] In fact, access to value-added food and leisure activities related to eating has become an indicator of upward mobility.

Those who do not enjoy the same level of privilege as their peers, due to social or economic circumstances, may feel like second-class citizens. The scenario changes completely. Depending on where they live, these persons may have access to a soup kitchen or a pantry that can provide food in case of emergencies, temporary lack of cash, or unemployment. They may also count on forms of support provided at the local, regional, or national level, such as free food for children and pregnant women, free lunches at school for students, food distributions, or financial aid to ensure sufficient *nutrition* for them and their families. They may have recourse to forage, hunt, or garden to supplement their diet. They may rely on their social and family networks to get extra food when needed, or they may have credit in the stores where they regularly shop. If they are members of an immigrant community, they may enjoy resources and solidarity that, although limited, can push them through a rough patch. At times, none of that may be available. *Hunger* and less extreme—but not less damaging for that—forms of food insecurity are not a rare occurrence, even if in the Global North they too often remain invisible or ignored.

Political dynamics that negotiate personal, communal, national, and international interests and priorities are also relevant in determining food environments. Attempts to introduce labeling regulations on foods containing *genetically modified organisms* (GMOs), which would allow consumers to express their preferences through their shopping choices, have been defeated in the United States. The justification against labeling is that such norms would impose a financial burden on producers, who ultimately would pass it on to consumers in the forms of higher prices. In the European Union (EU), citizens instead have expressed strong opinions against the production and consumption of GMOs, despite their governments' more flexible positions. Such consumers' preferences have a direct impact on the agricultural policies elsewhere. Pressure from international nongovernmental organizations (NGOs), nonprofit organizations, and the EU have led most African governments (with the exception of South Africa, Egypt, and a few others) to avoid or at least limit the introduction of GMO crops.

Personal choices and the responsibilities that come with them are often mentioned when state or national governments try to impose controls, restrictions, or taxes on what its citizens may buy in an attempt to limit the consumption of items that are likely to have a negative impact on public health. In the United States, proposals to tax sugared drinks have been met with objections against the "nanny state," based on the argument that everybody should enjoy the freedom to make their own decisions and that such taxes would heavily hit low-income populations who may appreciate sugared drinks as one of the few pleasures they can afford. Furthermore, such attempts may be criticized as efforts by well-meaning but often elitist reformers to interfere with other people's lifestyles. In other countries, such as Japan, China, India, or Italy, citizens instead tend to expect their governments to take the lead in such matters, which are widely considered a responsibility of public authorities. As in the GMO case, the influence of the food industry in the political debate is easy to detect.

As remote from us these political issues may seem, they actually reach all aspects of our lives, whether we realize it or not. Food is more than just a way to provide fuel to our bodies, especially in the consumer culture in which we are increasingly enmeshed. Although obviously crucial for survival, eating cannot be considered only as an expression of biological necessities and a natural, trivial aspect of our daily routine. Even the most cursory exploration of our habits and preferences as consumers prompts us to realize that food is complicated. It is profoundly entangled with

Food is more than
just a way to provide
fuel to our bodies,
especially in the
consumer culture
in which we are
increasingly enmeshed.

economic dynamics, social structures, and power negotiations that determine where our products come from, how they get to us, why we have access to those and not others, and where they end up if we don't buy them or throw them away. Undoubtedly, food has an immediate and unavoidable impact on who we are and how we live. My daily food choices as an Italian living in the United States are likely to be at least partly different from those of my peers in my native Rome, despite our shared background. They are also definitely different from those of past generations of less privileged immigrants that left Italy in search of a better future in the United States, Venezuela, or Australia.

Shaping Our Preferences

We embrace food as a constitutive element of our cultural and social identities as individuals and community members, wherever we live and whatever our access to food may be. We can and do use food consumption to express the traits that define our personalities and distinctiveness; one can, say, be white, conservative, gay, obsessed with exercise, eager to avoid gluten, or ready to gobble down Mexican food while asking for a higher border wall, in all sorts of combinations. Although self-asserting, the emphasis on these attitudes also make us easier targets for the focused marketing of companies that are increasingly interested in satisfying our inclinations while giving us the illusion of being unique in our *tastes* and choices—at a cost, of course.

The elements that determine consumers' preferences and behaviors are numerous and interwoven in interesting and unexpected ways, depending not only on free will but also on large, more complicated structural issues. Whether we want it or not, whether we are aware of it or not, by simply shopping, cooking, and eating, we connect ourselves to complex *supply networks*, institutions, and organizations that extend well beyond our families, our immediate communities, and even the countries in which we reside. We may feel increasingly detached from traditions and local customs as we become exposed to values, practices, and material objects from every corner of the world. These processes of globalization, experienced as progressively faster and uncontrollable, generate a sense of both freedom and anxiety. We enjoy having easy access to sushi and tacos, but we may fear losing ourselves and our culinary identities. This tension is frequently used for political goals: in 2011, in Italy, an anti-immigrant party printed posters that proclaimed "No to couscous—yes to polenta," while distributing huge quantities of the corn-based dish on the street as an expression of local identity, in opposition to the food of the North African and Middle Eastern immigrants.[2] In 2015, in Poland, despite the great success of foreign restaurants among the population, from pizza to kebab, a former politician was accused of elitist cosmopolitanism and lack of national pride for consuming octopus, a foreign and unusual food for most Poles, during a high-profile dinner.[3]

Consumption is an intensely social practice, and although it is based on individual behaviors, it is not limited to them. The environments in which we are raised, with their biases, prejudices, taboos, and partialities— due to a multiplicity of factors, including religion, ethnicity, class, and education—profoundly influence our preferences, our actions, and the way we think about what's good to eat. Social status and financial security also impact not only what we eat, but also how we think about it. Food can reflect different, even opposing values and priorities. For food scholar Margot Finn, for instance, the more liberal portion of the professional middle class in the United States expresses its preferences through what she defines as "the ideology of the food revolution," built around the four axes of sophistication, thinness, purity, and cosmopolitanism.[4] In other words, favorite foods in this worldview tend to be "gourmet," relatively difficult to acquire and definitely different from mass-produced fare; healthy and conducive to avoiding obesity; natural and free from scientific manipulations perceived as dangerous, from pesticides and fertilizers to genetic engineering; and authentic, reflecting other cultures and practices that are at the same time appreciated for bringing new flavor to mainstream habits and considered available to various degrees of appropriation and exploitation, including "slumming" to ethnic restaurants and neighborhoods. Although Finn's analysis focuses on the United States, similar attitudes can be observed among the upwardly mobile middle classes of Western Europe, Brazil, or India, among others.

In Finn's opinion, these ideals often reflect the not always overt but determinate attempt of the "food elites"—from affluent consumers to media influencers and marketers—to promote and at times to impose categories of taste, forms of selectivity, and practices of self-restraint that not everybody may subscribe to. Although it cannot be denied that at times the efforts to change food systems have recognizable class undertones, individuals and communities of all social backgrounds may choose to work toward greater health, purity, and cultural diversity in what they eat due to their own concerns. Engagement with food politics is not the exclusive domain of those with certain levels of education, social clout, or financial affluence. In Gaza, urban gardening is supported as a tool to reduce dependency on external aid.[5] In Cape Town, municipal land has been made available to low-income women to grow their own food.[6] In Detroit as in Manila, in São Paulo as in Mumbai, efforts to create community gardens, enhance food access, and improve children's nutrition are not uniquely the reflection of elite priorities but have been at the forefront of social and political action among groups that have suffered long-lasting disadvantages because of gender, race, and ethnicity.

Consumer Communities

The growing complexity of the social dynamics determining food choices makes the job of marketers and advertisers increasingly more difficult. In the past, mass production allowed for accessibility and affordability of products, as well as their wide distribution, and was embraced as a sign of progress. Nowadays it is increasingly replaced by the fragmentation of consumers among smaller and smaller segments that are supposed to reflect personal predilections. Everybody feels different and special and expects products catered to his or her inclinations. In reality, these allegedly individual preferences end up overlapping with emerging, temporary, always fluid, almost tribal formations congealing around cultural sensibilities, social identifications, political sensibilities, and dietary and health concerns. Personal stories connect with larger narratives to generate new identities. These consumer communities transcend national boundaries, feeding on global and widely shared repositories of ideas, images, and practices. Brooklyn-style cafés may be found in Warsaw, Rio de Janeiro, and Mumbai, with similar designs and menus, despite local variations. Instagram and other social media are shaping expectations about what good food and nice restaurants should look like, making them less diverse, regardless of their geographical location. Such dynamics complicate any definition of a "developing" or "developed" society, as class, ethnic, and racial distinctions may be as relevant as residence in a specific country. Middle-class youth around the world embrace occupations, from butchering to liquor distillation, that until recently would have carried a working-class stigma but are now given new prestigious status as forms of artisanal creativity. Wine enthusiasts share a complex vocabulary that transcends languages. These actors share with other food lovers around the world a common approach and homologous categories of taste, made exclusive and relevant in terms of status and expertise and experienced in appropriate environments and among peers who share the same outlook on food and its sociocultural relevance, regardless of where they live.

In such an interconnected landscape, a marketing campaign can be appreciated by some and loathed by others. In 2011, many Italians were horrified when the late Gualtiero Marchesi, a chef widely considered one of the fathers of contemporary Italian cuisine, teamed up with McDonald's to create sandwiches that showcased Italian products, with the blessing of the minister of agriculture.[7] When R&B sensation Mary J. Blige appeared in a television commercial for Burger King, singing about fried chicken wraps, the campaign was criticized for playing into racist stereotypes and was quickly taken off the air.[8] Even the political inclinations of the CEOs of food companies may influence product perception among shoppers. Which party do they support? What are their positions regarding important social and cultural issues? The American fast food company Chick-fil-A has provoked the indignation of liberals because of its leadership's opposition to same-sex marriage. Amazon recently acquired the upscale Whole Foods Market grocery store chain, creating confusion and discomfort in many of the chain's clients who had embraced its social and sustainability priorities, even if it meant paying premium prices. Technology is increasingly central to marketing efforts. The *Internet of Things* (IoT)—the connection of devices exchanging data through the internet—is expanding. Home security systems can be controlled through cell phones, and voice-activated "virtual assistants" routinely help to send emails and regulate heating systems. IoT innovations could improve the efficiency of food distribution networks, enhance product traceability, and establish connections among cooking appliances, refrigerators, and food vendors. By monitoring these flows of data, including those online purchases made through specialized websites, and mining web search histories through cookies, marketers receive a constant flow of information about the choices and behaviors of individual customers, for whom they are able to tailor personalized communication and advertising. Food production is trying to appear less an industrial and mass-oriented outcome of factory labor and more the result of labors of love, more local than global. Consumers' satisfaction is made to appear as a priority for food businesses. However, you only need scratch the surface to realize that the main goal of food businesses is still profit.

The fragmentation of interests and preferences among consumers is both reflected and amplified by the relevance food has acquired in contemporary media over the past two decades. Formats like Master Chef and Top Chef have colonized TV in many countries, with very little change from place to place. Food films have become a successful genre in the United States, Japan, India, France, Spain, and Brazil, to mention just a few.[9] Food has invaded the internet through specialized websites and social media platforms that allow users around the world to post information and pictures about their meals and the dishes they cook, exchange tips about restaurants and stores, and discuss food-related issues.

All over the world, these media interactions are largely dominated by what is sometimes referred to as *food porn*: a set of visual and auditory strategies—shots, camera movements, slow motion, lighting, sound, and editing—that aim to offer images of food so pleasurable and attractive that viewers lust after it, even when they are excluded from consumption. Just as in pornography, graphic, acoustic, and narrative components are meant to reproduce the physical acts of eating and savoring for spectators, often achieving comparable levels of excitement—without actual satisfaction. Media also provide a perfect environment for global *food fads* to emerge, develop, and whither, from diets with little or no scientific base to moral panics and trends regarding ingredients, dishes, and techniques. The marketability of food, its pervasive and lucrative representations on television and in magazines, advertising, literature, and a plethora of self-help and recipe books, suggest that narratives about cooking, eating, and—more recently—producing food constitute a highly charged arena in which cultural, social, economic, and political tensions converge.

Although food has historically been used as a tool to exert influence and power and to distinguish ethnic and religious belonging, as well as social class and wealth, it was not a common topic for public debates or even polite conversations and educated discussions. Among the exceptions were small circles of culinary professionals, bohemians that enjoyed exploring cheap and exotic establishments (often run by immigrants), and gourmets—a category that was often the target of ridicule and pointed critique. When Alexandre Grimod de la Reynière singlehandedly invented a new genre by writing his *Almanach des gourmands* and his commentaries about restaurants and stores in Napoleonic Paris, he raised quite a few eyebrows among his peers. Similarly, when the *New York Times* decided to hire Craig Claiborne in 1957 as its first full-time, all-expenses-covered food critic, it took some time for him to gain the respect of his colleagues. The cosmopolitan and educated upper and middle classes around the world are now comfortable showing off familiarity with the newest superfoods, discussing the advantages (or drawbacks) of different *nutrients*, products, and diets. They brag about the last visit to a trendy up-and-coming restaurant and are proud of being chummy with a celebrity chef or famous food producers. Taking pictures of what is cooked or eaten and dissecting the latest episode of a favorite cooking show (which are often global formats) are acceptable activities across classes. Hollywood celebrities are not immune: Gwyneth Paltrow ventured into food and eating with her upscale company Goop, while Mark Wahlberg launched the Wahlburgers chain of restaurants. Food has moved from a crucial necessity and a fundamental economic resource that used to run almost invisibly in the background—except in the case of crisis—to the forefront of media and popular culture, social movements, and political considerations.

Consumers as Citizens in the Food System

Food's newly central presence in all sorts of everyday conversations is intensified by the fact that because everybody eats, we all consider ourselves experts. Precisely for this reason, this book will tackle the sprawling topic of food from a consumer's standpoint, starting from our own everyday experiences and then following the connections that tie us through wider and wider networks to the food system at various scales—from the local to the global. We will see that we can be much more than consumers: we can reclaim our role as citizens.

Without realizing it, a child that unwraps her favorite chocolate candy, anywhere in the world, is unknowingly entangled in intricate and wide-reaching linkages that connect her to stores, distributors, manufacturers, food scientists, nutritionists, food importers and exporters, crops producers and agrobusinesses, agronomists, botanists, biologists, and, lately, climatologists. That's not all: tax and custom agencies, all levels of government, international organizations, and many other actors, more or less invisible to the average consumer, influence the shape and the nature of the networks in which they participate. In the case of the chocolate bar, all these stakeholders determine where the cocoa is grown, in what varieties, and by whom; how much farmers are paid and in which conditions they work; how cocoa beans are bought, transported, and distributed across the globe; who turns the cocoa into chocolate and how; how the chocolate is manufactured, packaged, marketed, and distributed; who has access to it and at what price it is sold: in other words, who wins and who loses, who profits, and who is exploited in the food system.

Of course, nobody particularly wants to think about all that when they just want to enjoy some chocolate, especially if the candy satisfies a craving or it is a gift from a loved one. Moreover, consumption of sweets may come with heavy emotional luggage due to health or body image issues. Understandably, we tend to focus on the product at hand and the pleasure that it brings us. There's nothing wrong with that! However, being aware of the dynamics that support the food system can empower us, not only as individual consumers but also as citizens and members of all sorts of social formations that range from the local to the regional, national, and international. Looking at the bigger picture is likely to help us make better-informed decisions in terms of not only personal preferences and political outlooks, but also more active social participation. If we acknowledged that our purchasing choices ("voting with our wallets") are not enough to solve all issues, we would probably be more amenable to taking collaborative actions, beyond our personal spheres. Understanding the present could help us determine which future we want to live in, one that better reflects our preferences but also responds to the needs of larger segments of the world population.

The goal of this book is to identify the aspects of food systems that have great impact on our everyday lives, whether we are aware of it or not. In fact, many central and critical issues in the contemporary food system remain largely invisible to the public at large. They are harder to grasp because they are systemic, often originate in long-term historical dynamics, and have global ramifications that require familiarity with the complexities of international affairs to be fully understood. Our desire for convenience and access to cheap food may have unwanted consequences in terms of how supply chains and distribution networks are structured, influencing what's grown, how it's grown, and how it gets to us. For this reason, the book will take readers beyond experiences that directly and obviously affect them, to highlight more intricate connections that may not be immediately evident, in part because some involved parties—usually those with financial and political power—have an interest in hiding their actions and their interests.

Each chapter highlights tensions and contradictions that underlie current discussions about food, as well as their consequences for us as consumers and citizens, even when the issues may appear distant and unrelated to everyday life: the connections between climate change and agriculture; the impact of technology and intellectual property; the *financialization of food commodities* and its consequences on worldwide food crises; the expansion of biofuel manufacturing, with the possible reduction of land available for food production; and land acquisitions

Our desire for convenience and access to cheap food may have unwanted consequences in terms of how supply chains and distribution networks are structured, influencing what's grown, how it's grown, and how it gets to us.

in developing countries. Such aspects of the food system cannot be dealt with from just a local or national perspective because they touch on issues ranging from planetary environmental changes to international trade and economic development—which in turn are closely connected with political debates about nationalism, populism, identity, and migrations.

One of the core arguments of this book is that the food system is increasingly global. However, we inevitably look at it from a specific location, which in my case and in the case of most readers is the Global North. It is not an easy task to define the consumer from whose point of view this book looks at various aspects of food experiences. The role of consumers, their identity, and their participation in the food system vary greatly from place to place and from moment to moment. Beyond the growing segmentation of the market, consumers differ in terms of sex, gender, age, location, culture, education, ethnicity, religion, income, and social status, to mention just a few differentiating factors. Even taking into consideration the obvious differences, however, when it comes to preferences, categories of taste, and expectations, now widely shared through travel, media, and direct contact, a middle-class shopper in Bangalore may have more in common with her peers in Lima, Athens, and Lagos than with individuals from lower-income groups living in her city.

It was necessary to make choices in writing this book; taking position and embracing a point of view is inevitable. The book is written for readers who—wherever they are located—are at least moderately invested in what they eat from the point of view of price, convenience, sensory qualities, connection to one's preferences, and health. Such individuals, although more focused on their personal actions and choices and not particularly concerned about the confusing economics and politics of the food system, are likely to be at least somewhat troubled by issues of environmental sustainability, labor exploitation, hunger, ethics, and justice, especially when they realize that their behaviors and personal decisions have direct and indirect consequences.

In other words, this book is for readers who may not always be thinking about social and political issues, but who still want to make choices without renouncing their roles, rights, and responsibilities as citizens. We can decide to be spectators or to embrace more active, hands-on attitudes in building a future we may be happier to live in—a future in which we have a greater say about what is grown and produced and how, making sure that land, water, and air remain clean and fruitful for generations to come; in which hunger is a bad memory and everybody has stable access to healthy and nutritious food; and in which technology works for everybody's well-being, rather than turning into a tool for few to become richer and more powerful.

In democratic societies, we tend to believe that we hold the power to impose our preferences on product manufacturers and service providers. We are convinced that we vote with our wallets and that our votes count. The apparent impact of social media and consumers' outrage on the marketing decisions of large corporations increases this sense of agency. When we are unhappy with any aspect of what we eat, where we buy our food, and how much we pay, we focus on personal choices and their impact on the market, believing in the effectiveness of the law of supply and demand. We all have a stake in food, but we are often wrapped in illusions about what we can do as individual consumers to achieve a better, healthier, more sustainable, more just food system. Moreover, not all consumers are in a position to assert their choices through the market. As a matter of fact, millions are victims of global dynamics in which they have no say. Understanding how food is produced, processed, distributed, marketed, consumed, and even wasted or disposed of has never been more important. Thinking critically about the present inevitably leads us to question the status quo and to imagine different scenarios. The future of the food system is in our hands, not only as consumers but also as citizens.

The future of the food system is in our hands, not only as consumers but also as citizens.

MAKING SENSE OF FOOD SYSTEMS

It would be much harder to get my day started if I did not have a cup of coffee, tea, or, if I am feeling decadent, hot chocolate. The aroma of dark roast beans (sorry, not a fan of light roasts) that fills the apartment tells me it is time to get moving. I know it will not be my only cup of the day, but it is the one I cannot do without. Born and raised in Italy, a big savory breakfast is not usually my first choice: yogurt with cereals (not the cloyingly sweet ones), oatmeal with jam and almonds, or—even better—a fresh cornetto pastry does it for me. Of course, I'm adaptable. When I was traveling in Japan, I, like many locals, enjoyed grilled fish and miso soup with rice as my first meal of the day, beautifully served in deceptively rough tableware. During my years in China, I must admit I never quite got used to the very common breakfast of rice congee, often served with pickled vegetables, eggs, or whatever was left from the previous night's dinner. Now that I often do research in Poland, I don't mind their *jajecznica* scrambled eggs with kielbasa, tomatoes, and cucumbers. What is familiar and comforting differs quite substantially from place to place. Wherever I eat, though, I need my coffee—or at least a strong tea. Such excitants are relatively convenient and cheap, especially—but not exclusively—in the Global North. Those same items may feel luxurious elsewhere, particularly to less affluent consumers.

I may be sleepy or thrilled about the day or nervous about an impending work task or sad because of something that happened the night before—so though I savor my breakfast, I rarely feel very inclined to think about where the drink I am consuming *really* comes from. That is not uncommon among consumers. Depending on our level of engagement with what we eat, our horizon may limit itself to the kitchen pantry or the fridge, especially if we are not in charge of shopping, or may extend beyond our homes to the stores, supermarkets, street merchants, and trucks from which we may purchase our groceries or which provide a convenient delivery service directly to our doorstep.

Most of the time, we are not particularly concerned about where our food was grown or processed and how it got from there to where we bought it. We tend to be oblivious to the complex infrastructures that underlie contemporary distribution systems, from technologies such as refrigerated transportation to warehousing logistics. The child who enjoyed her chocolate candy in the last chapter is likely to have very little investment in understanding the provenance of her treat. Similarly, a busy office worker gulping down coffee all day long at her desk may not probably care that much about where her java comes from, nor would a British miner sipping hot tea out of a thermos during his break muse about the source and history of the leaves steeping in his drink.

Of course, we are suddenly—and painfully—made aware of the provenance of food when disruptions such as labor strikes, riots, disease outbreaks, fuel shortages, or natural disasters cut us off from food's invisible distribution networks. The fragility of the whole system may reveal itself even in the most modern cities of the Global North. New Yorkers experienced fear of food scarcity in 2012 after hurricane Sandy, when no gas was available for trucks to make deliveries to stores, electricity outages made refrigerating and cooking food very difficult, and flooding in some neighborhoods forced people to turn to family, friends, and charities for food. Knowing where our food comes from, and how, is important to us as consumers and as citizens, allowing us to make more careful choices. In this chapter, we will go beyond our daily experiences to explore the global food system and the structures, flows, and stakeholders that compose it. We will also examine how supply networks function; we will see how they

We are suddenly—and painfully—made aware of the provenance of food when disruptions such as labor strikes, riots, disease outbreaks, fuel shortages, or natural disasters cut us off from food's invisible distribution networks.

are shaped not only by economic and logistic factors, but also by cultural, social, and political dynamics.

The Local and the Global

Wherever we live, whatever portion of our budget we spend on food, however we experience our meals, it is quite likely that much of what we eat is harvested or slaughtered in distant places we are not familiar with. Our food is often prepared, processed, and packaged in plants the operations of which we may not understand, to be distributed through intricate networks spanning from the local to the global. The final products are eventually sold to us through different channels as ingredients and prepackaged items. We can also enjoy them prepared and cooked in restaurants, cafes, cafeterias, and other places of public consumption.

Such complexity is not limited to products such as bananas or pineapples, which obviously are harvested in tropical and equatorial locations. Our shrimp may be farmed and frozen in Vietnam. Our grapes may come from Chile. Our coffee may be grown and harvested in Nicaragua, roasted in Germany, and distributed in Canada. The feet of chickens raised and slaughtered in the United States often end up in China. The cookies I enjoy with my coffee when I am in Italy may be made with flour, butter, milk, and sugar imported from other countries. The wheat from which the flour was milled, possibly originating in Canada or the Ukraine, may be the result of breeding experiments conducted in anonymous laboratories in far-flung sites and patented by a transnational corporation with its headquarters in Paris, New York, or Shanghai. The factory that manufactured the cookies may be around the corner from my apartment in Rome or located across national borders, even if a local brand packages the product in familiar ways. Living in the countryside does not provide better assurance of fresh, local food; in fact, rural consumers very often have little access to products from their own area and are forced (and sometimes prefer) to buy from stores or even big-box supermarkets that purvey cheap and convenient goods from remote places. Anonymous commodities then can be transformed into familiar meals and comfort food through the preparation, care, and emotional labor of consumers.

The complexities of production and distribution are not necessarily negative, as they ensure easy and affordable access to food for large segments of the world's population. As consumers, we tend to appreciate fruits and vegetables regardless of the seasons and their provenance. It's hard to complain about having flour, sugar, salt, and all sort of groceries within arm's reach at any given time. That was not always the case, and it still is not in many areas of the world. It's a luxury that until recently only the richest were able to afford. It's important to resist any temptation to embrace nostalgia for an idyllic, preindustrial past that never existed while ignoring the hardships that most humans have experienced throughout history to produce, acquire, and prepare food. However, the mechanisms that make food convenient, cheap, and available year-round remain obscure. What do low production costs mean in terms of the wages and safety of those employed in the food industry? What do the people who produce our food eat?

We are so enmeshed in this sprawling circulation of anonymous ingredients and foods that we may rejoice when we have access to groceries the provenance of which we can pinpoint: fresh mushrooms an aunt foraged for us, vegetables from a nearby farm (urban or rural, depending on where we live), bread from a baker we are on a first-name basis with. Growing segments of shoppers, in particular those with larger disposable incomes, are willing to pay premium prices for foodstuffs with specific places of origin, produced according to traditional methods, and distributed more directly to consumers. These shifting preferences are still mostly limited to cosmopolitan, mostly urban, and relatively educated and affluent consumers from the Global North. However, they have become visible enough to be a target of satire, as in a skit from the US TV show *Portlandia*, in which a waitress tells the life story of a free-range chicken to increasingly concerned

The mechanisms that make food convenient, cheap, and available year-round remain obscure. What do low production costs mean in terms of the wages and safety of those employed in the food industry? What do the people who produce our food eat?

customers, providing detailed information—including the bird's name—and even a picture. Such predilections are becoming common among upwardly mobile middle classes around the world. In Poland, regional and traditional foods are increasingly available in stores and at food fairs and culinary events, after years of sushi and risotto constituting the epitome of cosmopolitanism and refinement. In Rio de Janeiro, various organizations are striving to bring food from nearby producers to urban shoppers, formerly cut off from direct provisioning, and to create direct connections among them. These kinds of products provide an alternative to commodities that, though usually cheaper, more accessible, and more convenient, do not ensure the same transparency, especially when marketers wrap them in nostalgia. We are all familiar with industrial ice cream pretending to be lovingly manufactured in quaint, old parlors, or precut frozen vegetables allegedly coming from green valleys, duly represented on the plastic packaging in all their splendid greenery. Knowing where what we eat *really* comes from is becoming increasingly important.

These shifts in consumers' preferences have led, among other consequences, to the development of *geographical indications*, a category of intellectual property—regulated by a World Trade Organization (WTO) treaty—that provides visibility and protection to specialties such as champagne from France, Parmigiano-Reggiano from Italy,

Darjeeling tea from India, and tequila from Mexico. The premium prices of these products are predicated on their connection with a precise (and circumscribed) place of origin and codified production procedures.[1] The legal category of geographical indications, in fact, builds on and expands the concept of *terroir*, which emerged in France in the second half of the nineteenth century. The idea of terroir connects quality, flavor, and other tangible characteristics of a product with the environment from where it originates—including soil and climate—and the practical know-how established over time by the communities that inhabit that same environment.

Looking Back in Time

It is not coincidental that the concept of terroir developed precisely at a time when France was undergoing its industrial revolution. Large groups of countryside dwellers were moving to the cities, where jobs in modern manufacturing sectors were abundant. Quite suddenly, individuals and families that were used to directly producing at least part of their food and buying the rest from neighbors and sellers that they knew personally found themselves instead in urban environments, removed from the places where food was grown and separated from the family and community networks that ensured access to fresh, local fare.

This sense of loss and anxiety was intensified by counterfeits and adulterations that at times had fatal consequences: not infrequently, chalk was added to milk or sawdust to bread. Cities found themselves forced to provide *food safety* protection to their inhabitants, especially those from the upper classes who were more vocal and could exert more pressure on local authorities. Those interventions are at the origin of the policies that cities still adopt to address contemporary concerns about food quality. On the one hand, cities started building more spacious and salubrious markets that offered a valid alternative to small stores and street vendors (also allowing more control and easier taxation). On the other hand, tighter quality controls were established and specialized laboratories were founded to verify and guarantee the content of food products.[2]

It is at this time that in the most advanced Western European countries, the United States, and, later, Japan, the food system changed radically, shifting from local to national and international networks that increased the distance and separation between producers and consumers. As a matter of fact, being able to have access to and afford products coming from far away was experienced as a mark of social distinction. Such transformations were ushered by advances in agriculture. New varieties of seeds and animal species selected for sturdiness and higher yields were introduced, while the mechanization of agricultural processes increased. In the twentieth century, the use of fertilizers and pesticides became widespread, allowing the intensification of cultivations, with more abundant crops growing faster and more efficiently. These advances were spread among farmers by specialized public agencies, often connected with research centers and universities.

Such a revolution would not have been possible without new forms of transportation supported by increasingly efficient engines—powered by steam and later by fossil fuels—that reduced the time to move goods from one point to another within nations and beyond. Fast ships could easily carry merchandise along rivers and across seas, whereas railroads crisscrossed continents, ensuring a more capillary, efficient, and swift acquisition and distribution of foodstuffs. Many technologies were launched and developed as part of war efforts, starting with the *appertization* process (which allows for preservation in jars and cans) during the Napoleonic Wars in the early nineteenth century. These advances were further compounded by refrigeration, which over time changed not only the way food was produced, warehoused, and shipped, but also consumers' expectations about freshness and their relationships with seasonality.[3]

Inevitably, such changes allowed for a greater specialization in food production. It made sense to grow certain crops in locations that were more favorable and provided a comparative advantage in terms of soil, climate, availability of labor, and proximity to large markets. The expenses connected with long-range transportation were compensated for with lower production costs at the origin. In addition, new technologies allowed for economies of scale that further reduced the costs of production.

However, the investment necessary for machines and infrastructure increasingly disadvantaged small farmers who did not have access to capital and financing, favoring concentration and further mechanization. Due to the need for liquidity and investment funds to launch and maintain large enterprises, as well as the need to secure sales at acceptable prices in cases of natural disasters, wars, or other unexpected events, farmers took to *hedging*—that is, signing contracts for future deliveries at a price agreed upon before harvest. Such agreements, which distributed the risks between sellers and buyers, facilitated the introduction of food commodities such as wheat, pork, and beef to the stock market, where the contracts could be sold, bought, and speculated on.

The nineteenth and early twentieth centuries also saw colonialism reach its apex, with imperial powers imposing their priorities over the productive systems of their colonies (see chapter 7). Materials were extracted in subjugated territories at low cost and shipped to the imperial metropolis to be turned into value-added merchandise, which was in turn sold back to the colonies for a profit. For instance, after new technologies were developed to produce cooking oil from peanuts, the French government promoted a shift from rice, a traditional staple, to peanuts in its West African colonies. Peanuts were shipped to France and turned into oil that was then sold at high prices in West Africa, where rice was now imported from the French colonies in Southeast Asia. Such structures of domination and exploitation, which food system experts Harriet Friedman and Philip McMichael defined as the first global *food regime*, were predominant between 1870 and the 1930s.[4] They developed out of the explorations that European countries embarked on from the fifteenth century, followed by the conquest of territories into which commercial crops from all over the world were introduced to support the economic growth of the colonial powers. Coffee was taken out of the Middle East and planted in the Caribbean, Central and South America, Africa, and Asia. Vanilla and cocoa were brought from the New World to tropical areas around the world. Colonies became stuck in the production of commodities at increasingly low prices, without the ability to develop local industries; manufactured products were often imported from the metropolis, wrapped in an aura of modernity and sophistication that made them more valuable and pricier than the local foodstuffs. The consequence was that traditional crops that required intense labor and provided relatively lower yields–such as fonio in West Africa, amaranth in Mexico, or quinoa in the Andes—were not only replaced by crops

imposed by the metropolis to support industrial production but also shunned as symbols of backwardness and
poverty. Increases in yield and efficiency favored *monocultures* that have been threatening *agrobiodiversity* ever
since, limiting the variety of crops and food available to
consumers. The independence and decolonization movements in the second half of the twentieth century have
not succeeded in changing these global dynamics. Forms
of quasi-colonial exploitation still exist, exacerbated by
a tendency toward greater concentration and consolida-
tion in the food system. To this day, commercial crops
constitute crucial sources of income for developing countries, despite their low prices—such as cocoa in Côte
d'Ivoire and Ghana, bananas in Ecuador and St. Vincent
and the Grenadines, and coffee in Indonesia, Honduras,
and Uganda.

World War II deeply influenced how populations
around the world experienced food availability in terms
of expectations, rations, public interventions, technology,
and logistics. According to Friedman and McMichaels, this
determined the second food regime, in full swing between
the 1950s and the 1970s, when the United States acquired
a central position in international exchanges by using its
agricultural surpluses to support first the Western countries that were recovering after the war and later Eastern
European and developing countries. In the political atmosphere caused by the Cold War, big firms participated first

in food aid and later in the efforts of the green revolution, the goal of which was to spread modern agricultural methods, technologies, and high-yield varieties in developing countries (see chapter 5). This involvement allowed large transnational corporations to capture growing segments of the global food markets. Since the 1950s, they have constantly expanded and absorbed competitors both among upstream firms, which provide inputs such as machinery, fertilizers, and seeds to agribusinesses, and among downstream firms that operate in food manufacturing and marketing.

The push toward deregulation in the 1980s ushered what may be considered a third food regime, based on free global trade, easy movement of financial capitals, and the growing centrality of intellectual property—from trademarks to scientific innovations (see chapter 5). A few companies now control international seed production, agricultural machinery, commodity trading, meat processing and packaging, and food processing. The agricultural chemical and seed sector, for instance, has recently seen a sudden wave of mergers: Dow Chemical Co. integrated with DuPont Pioneer; ChemChina took over Syngenta; and as of the time of writing, Bayer is buying Monsanto. Such historical transformations, as abstract as they may seem, have profoundly influenced what ends up on the fields and on our plates, regardless of who we are and where we live.

Big-box supermarkets can impose their terms on farmers and manufacturers around the world, pushing prices down and forcing smaller retails competitors out of the market. There are plenty of food producers and final consumers, but very few companies in between that can connect them, both within each individual country and globally. Author and activist Raj Patel observes that "the process of shipping, processing, and trucking food across distances requires a great deal of capital—you need to be rich to play this game. It is also a game that has economies of scale ... when the number of companies controlling the gateways from farmers to consumers is small, this gives them market power both over the people who grow the food and the people who eat it."[5] Large transnational corporations such as Nestle, Unilever, Coca-Cola, Danone, Associated British Foods, and Mondelez control most of the brands that consumers around the world can easily recognize.

Understanding Supply Networks

The swift process of industrialization that started in the nineteenth century has profoundly transformed the preferences, habits, and eating patterns of consumers not only in Western Europe, North America, and Japan, but also in the Global South, where such dietary models, although not necessarily healthier, are increasingly perceived as expressions of progress and economic success. The Chinese and Indian middle classes now eat more meat and dairy, considered higher-status foods and symbols of wealth and Western modernity. In the early 1980s, the Chinese consumed around 10 kg of meat (mostly pork) per person—but in 2015, the amount was already closer to 60 kg, with an increase in beef and, above all, poultry.[6] The average annual growth rate of milk consumption in India has been 4.4 percent (8.0 percent for skim milk powder), concentrated above all among the wealthier segments of the population. Fast food and highly processed packaged products are ubiquitous.[7]

However, not everybody has access to the same quantity and types of food. The percentage of the household income spent on food varies not only from country to country, but also within countries. According to the World Economic Forum, in 2015 the average percentage of household income spent on food consumed at home in the United States was 6.4 percent (due to the widespread availability of prepared food in commercial venues). At the other end of the spectrum, Nigerian families spend 56.4 percent of their income on food consumed at home.[8] It seems there is a direct correlation between the level of industrialization of the food system and the affordability of food. However, there are also stark differences within countries. In 2017 in the United States, families in the bottom 20 percent in terms of wealth spent 34.1 percent of their income on total food expenditures (both at home and outside), whereas the top 20 percent spent less than 10 percent.[9] Food may be cheap, but that does not necessarily make it affordable.

The apparently infinite choices, the convenience, and the food accessibility that consumers in postindustrial societies enjoy today are neither the inevitable outcome of unstoppable scientific and social progress nor so stable as to be everlasting. They are the results of complex interactions among countless and diverse actors. Is it possible to pinpoint stakeholders, organizations, and institutions that decide what to grow, where, and in which quantities? How do supply networks determine what animal species and varieties are raised, how they are butchered, and how they get to your local store? How are processing, packaging, distribution, and sales of food products coordinated? What kind of interactions among scientists, research institutions, food industries, and consumers determine what technologies succeed and are widely adopted and which are discounted and forgotten? The innumerable, intricate, and interconnected supply networks that make these productive and economic functions possible constitute what we call a *food system*.

It isn't easy to follow an item from its point of origin to where it is sold, consumed, and disposed of because the actors involved go well beyond the individuals or companies that grow, manufacture, package, distribute, and sell food-stuffs. As in the case of the chocolate candy we described in the previous chapter, the multilayered connections among places, actors, and processes are extremely complex. Contemporary supply mechanisms are more similar to open-ended, shifting, and unstable multidimensional networks than to well-defined, monodirectional chains neatly joining subsequent phases from production to consumption.

Let's explore the supply network that brings apples to a Warsaw supermarket. When looking at the agricultural side, actors include biologists that maintain old varieties and select new ones. National and transnational corporations may have patented such varieties while agronomists devised cultivation techniques and engineers designed the machinery used for the harvest, sorting, and climate-controlled storage of their fruit. Farmers and the labor they hire interact with local authorities that determine or influence the use of land, with legal experts that may intervene on property issues, with bank officers making decisions about loans and investments, and with insur-ance agents evaluating risks ranging from yield failures to market price fluctuations and natural disasters. Both farmers and authorities at the local and national levels ne-gotiate with the European Union to obtain funds for rural development. This list, which could be further expanded, indicates how linkages go well beyond the field, the fruit, and the people who grow it, connecting the place where apples originate with disparate locations, stakeholders, and processes inside and outside Poland.

Similar complexity extends into processing and distribution to include food scientists that come up with new products and manufacturing methods for cider, snacks, or jams, as well as designers that work on packaging. Local and national officers make political choices in terms of taxes, regulations, public health, food safety, and subsidies, under the influence of lobbying groups, international trade, and diplomacy. Marketers and advertisers are tasked with selling the fruit, whereas cultural mediators like journalists and food critics may highlight specific varieties for their flavors or for their connections to Polish traditions. The network extends to truckers and transportation agents, warehouse managers and workers, and distributors, wholesalers, and supermarket buyers. Consumers, both as individuals and as members of organizations that include activist groups, consumers' associations, and fan clubs of specific products, eventually connect with garbage collectors, landfill operators, and in some cases recycling experts. Even foreign countries may have an impact on supply networks. When Russia occupied Crimea in 2014, the European Union imposed sanctions on Russia, which in turn limited imports of EU products in retaliation, including Polish apples. In reaction to the political events, Polish authorities prompted their citizens to eat apples as a form of patriotism.

Such a list of actors, factors, and processes may seem confusing because it connects very heterogeneous and seemingly unrelated elements. That is precisely the point: networks are difficult to assess in terms of neat and clear relations among components belonging to the same category, along well-determined phases of production. Addressing such complexity requires new approaches. To fully understand supply networks—and to be able to intervene on them—it is necessary to shift from linear thinking, merely following products through various phases from beginning to end along neatly organized *supply chains*, to systemic thinking. This shift implies reasoning in terms of nodes and links that are connected not only with the step before and after in the production process, but also in multiple, concurrent, and often unpredictable ways with apparently unrelated factors, other supply networks, and external players. In the case of the Polish apples, farmers turn out to be tied to diplomats, European Union officers, scientists, engineers, and activists, among others. It's quite likely that the farmers are aware of such connections thanks to media, their own information networks, and professional organizations.

Supply networks go well beyond human actors. They include and depend on natural environments and artificial ecologies; resources such as soil and water, fuel, and other inputs; infrastructures and designed spaces; and objects and technologies as diverse as computers, cell phones, refrigerators, freezers, cargo containers, forklifts, and warehousing pallets (see chapter 5). To make everything even more fluid, supply networks are not only composed by static elements but also shaped by the interactions and flows of diverse factors ranging from money to ideas, diseases, contaminants, and the weather.

Creating Value

Considering the intricacy of supply networks, it isn't easy for us as consumers to understand why things cost what they cost and where their worth comes from. The value we attribute to a product may or may not be reflected in the price, which is determined by many diverse factors. For instance, when it comes to chocolate, the final price we pay at the grocery store is the result of the sum of costs attributable to the inputs and services provided by various stakeholders along the chain. After the farmers are remunerated for the cocoa beans, other value is added by those who take care of collecting and transporting the beans, those processing and packaging them, the exporters and importers, the processors and manufacturers that turn cocoa into chocolate, the marketers and advertisers that promote the final product, and finally the distributors and the retailers that sell it. All actors are supposed to receive compensation for their contribution and the value they add toward the final product, although in some cases laborers—especially children—work in conditions of extreme exploitation, with little pay.[10]

The distribution of opportunities for value creation and profit is inevitably the result of power negotiations among the actors involved in the supply network, determining who has control over the most lucrative phases of production. In the case of chocolate, the greatest amount of value is created in the transformation of cocoa into chocolate and in its packaging, branding, marketing, and distribution. These phases usually take place in the Global North, where large food companies reap the largest benefits. Could those high-value-added activities be transferred closer to the areas of production? What if cooperatives of cocoa farmers could also process the beans? How much of the value added would they be able to capture? And what kind of structural, political, and economic changes in the supply network would be required to make this shift of value production possible? It's quite likely that big companies in developed countries would oppose such moves because they would affect the bottom line.

Such reflections are valid not only for transnational supply networks but also at the national and local levels. What percentage of the final price of vegetables does a farmer receive if she sells her products to an intermediary who then in turn sells to a wholesale market that in turn sells to retailers? How would her percentage increase if that farmer could sell directly to consumers? Of course, this shift would require finding customers and creating stable relationships—and that's what farmers' markets and CSA initiatives are for.

Because supply networks do not operate in isolation from each other, they may generate connections, synergies, and conflicts. Almond growers in Southern California, where little water is available, inevitably find themselves clashing with other food industries to secure water rights (and clashing with those who live in the area, who also need water). The runoff of fertilizers from agricultural fields that flows into rivers and eventually to the sea may create sustainability issues for industries such as fish farming or fishing. However, farmers who use fertilizers to increase their yields and improve their incomes do not cover the expenses necessary to clean polluted waters. These examples show how productive factors in one supply network can easily turn into negative externalities in others. By *negative externalities*, economists and environmental experts mean the side effects caused by one industry that are not taken into account in determining its costs of operation, such as pollution and public health issues generated by the production or consumption of certain goods. By not having to pay to take care of these side effects, an industry can keep its prices low, transferring costs to other actors or industries that unwillingly find themselves dealing with the externalities and, often, picking up the tab.

Scale and Distance

As a reaction to these issues and to the growing complexity of the global food system, the connections between urban centers and the nearby countryside in terms of infrastructures, social dynamics, and flows of goods—networks often referred to as *foodsheds*—have been playing an increasingly central role in building efficient, equitable, and sustainable food systems. It's important for people in Rome to have access to affordable, fresh food from nearby places they may be familiar with or they may get to know in the future, the same way dwellers of Lagos may enjoy vegetables and seafood from close-by areas, especially if the proximity allows for cheaper prices, as well as more stable and reliable supply connections. According to the World Bank, urban population worldwide has increased from around one billion in 1960 to over four billion in 2016—that is, from 33 percent to 54 percent of the total world population.[11] In the same period of time, the rural population only increased from 2 to 3.3 billion, which corresponds to an actual decrease from 66 percent to 45 percent of the total world population.[12] Not only do cities need farmers, but farmers need cities and large numbers of consumers to support their businesses. These concerns are legitimate and important. Being embedded in local food initiatives, from community gardens to CSAs, has great relevance in terms of civic society building and the creation of spaces outside the control of large, delocalized agribusinesses.

The notion that buying local is inherently better than accessing far-reaching networks has been gaining ground. Such a point of view has its most evident manifestation in the phenomenon of *locavorism*, which is the preference for or the exclusive consumption of food produced geographically close to consumers. We can also observe growing preoccupation with *food miles*, the distance over which products are transported from their origin to the final consumer. Such distance has obvious implications in terms of the amount of fuel used to move the merchandise and, therefore, in terms of carbon footprint, overall environmental impact, and, down the line, climate change. Importing water in plastic bottles from Fiji does not seem efficient.

However, one should avoid what urban planners Branden Born and Mark Purcell have defined as the *local trap*: the uncritical embrace of small-scale food networks as automatically more sustainable, more democratic, or more socially fair than far-reaching arrangements. Born and Purcell argue that the power balance among actors, their priorities, and the negotiations taking place among them are more relevant to determine the overall character of a supply network than its scale and dimension.[13] Furthermore, at times it may make better sense from the point of view of the environmental impact to obtain something from afar where that good can be produced more efficiently, rather than producing it locally at greater cost in terms of inputs and energy. In other words, in New Mexico, lamb from New Zealand may overall carry a smaller carbon footprint, despite the long-distance transportation and the use of large amounts of fossil fuels (food miles), than lamb raised in a nearby dry area, where huge amounts of water—a scarce input—must be used to provide good pastures for the animals. Of course, we could renounce all products that come from faraway locations; such choices, however, would be easier in temperate or Mediterranean climates than, say, in Scandinavia or Patagonia. Sustainability needs to be evaluated from economic and social points of view. Many factors determine what the best decision may be. If the Global North suddenly stopped importing bananas, coffee, and cocoa, among other products, to shift exclusively toward local crops, the economies of whole developing countries with incomes tied to agriculture would collapse.

Different Models, Different Choices

The internal choices of national governments often have repercussions for the structure and functioning of supply networks, well beyond their borders. Besides scale and distance, food politics and policies, which vary enormously from country to country, contribute to the complexity of the global food system. In places like the United States, competition and efficiency are supposed to give order to the market; in fact, vast segments of the population argue that the government should intervene as little as possible in food-related matters and let supply and demand take care of everything. When such an approach dominates in Congress and in the executive branch, due to the pressure of lobbying groups and large transnational corporations operating in food production and manufacturing, the result is deregulation from the point of view of labor issues, industry concentration and acquisitions, consumer protections, environmental safeguards, food safety, and *food security*. Contrary to its hands-off ideological proclamations, however, the US government employs a wide set of measures—the object of legislation known as the Farm Bill—to support its food production, from stabilization of farmers' incomes to direct payments, tariffs on imports, export subsidies, and acquisition programs for surplus products.

The United States is not the only country in which food production relies heavily on subsidies: this is the case in Japan and the European Union as well. However, there are differences in other aspects of food policies. In Western Europe, consumers tend to accept greater control and stricter regulatory measures from their governments if these can guarantee better quality, accessibility, affordability, and safety. As many of these regulations are now out of the hands of national governments, negotiated and voted on instead at the EU level, citizens often resent the interventions of a bureaucracy they consider disproportionate and out of their control.

Although most national food systems are more or less built on capitalist dynamics based on private initiative and the free play of supply and demand, governments still intervene to various degrees, as subsidies, quotas, and tariffs indicate. Control over alcohol (in many US states), meat (India), and staples (rice in much of Eastern Asia) blurs the distinctions between deregulated and coordinated capitalist food systems. In the past, experiments were made to establish a central control over all food production, distribution, and consumption, with the goals of ensuring sufficient and healthy food and increasing equality across the population. In war times, it was not unusual for governments to institute rations and coupons to better distribute limited resources among citizens of all social backgrounds. After World War I, the USSR introduced the collectivization of food production and manufacturing, and markets were centrally regulated. Other countries, such as China and Vietnam, followed its example. Although such experiments allowed for more egalitarian access to food across class differences, their inefficiencies also caused temporary scarcities and, in the worst cases, famines, as happened in Russia and the Ukraine in the mid-1930s and in China in the early 1960s. Even in the absence of crises, the limited availability of food, the long lines citizens had to endure on a regular basis to access a limited choice of products, and the relative luxury that party cadres seemed to enjoy contributed to delegitimize socialist regimes. Over time, changes happened either through planned reforms, as in China in the late 1970s when Deng Xiaoping ushered in the progressive liberalization of agricultural production and sales, or through the catastrophic implosion of the system, like in Russia and Eastern Europe in the early 1990s.

Although China has succeeded in ensuring food for most of its citizens, over time inequalities have emerged again between consumers in large urban areas, especially on the coasts, and farmers living in the interior and producing crops for the national market. The low prices that consumers pay are counterbalanced by the widespread poverty among food producers and the injustices they often deal with, from land expropriations to various forms of exploitation. Cuba has had to deal with the effects of both a long-term economic embargo, which limits its possibilities to export cash crops and to import food, and the consequences of the disintegration of the Communist bloc, which caused lack of fuel, agricultural inputs, and machinery. As a consequence, all of Cuban agriculture was forced to embrace forms of organic cultivation and permaculture. Following recent reforms, much food is being produced for the growing tourist sectors, and private citizens are allowed to turn their homes into *paladares*, small restaurants serving mostly traditional dishes.

The variety of structures and dynamics, the scope in terms of scale and distance, and the influence of factors ranging from social priorities to logistics all indicate that the global food system is not the inevitable result of an invisible hand or the expected outcome of natural endowments and productive resources, but rather the consequence of specific political and economic decisions at the local, national, and international levels. Choices in terms of land tenure legislation, market regulations, subsidies, and prices are the result of ongoing negotiations among stakeholders that may take different forms, from formal lobbying to informal influence or even corruption. The crucial question to ask to achieve a better understanding of the food system is simple: Who gains and who loses? And, in the most extreme cases, who ends up malnourished or hungry?

At times, basic economic competition is shrouded in the language of ethical and social principles, political partisanship, and even economic rationality. It is necessary to cut through the fog and follow the money to get to the bottom of noisy and at times overblown arguments. How do different groups express their manifest and hidden interests? How do they push their agendas ahead? These debates, heavily influenced by financial and political factors, have a profound impact on the well-being of citizens. In fact, as we will discuss in the next chapter, even health and nutrition are far from being free from controversies, entangled as they are in cultural categories, social taboos, economic interests, and discussions about the validity and trustfulness of science.

HEALTH AND NUTRITION

At a time in history when we, as citizens of postindustrial
societies, have unprecedented access to food (although
not everybody can actually afford it), we appear to be sad-
dled with growing anxieties about what we should actually eat and about what the food we eat does to us—and
for good reasons. Weight excess, poor diet, high fasting
plasma glucose levels, and alcohol-use disorders have
a profound impact on the well-being of individuals and
communities. Recent research identifies such food-related
issues among the major health risk factors for adults in
the United States.[1] Although this trend is clear in most
countries in the Global North, it's also emerging in the
rest of the world. Something is clearly wrong, and governments are taking action.[2]

Obesity, discussed with an increasing sense of urgency, has emerged as one of the most pressing issues.[3]

The World Health Organization (WHO) indicates it as a condition that increases the chances of developing non-communicable ailments such as diabetes, cardiovascular conditions, osteoarthritis, and even some cancers, including breast, ovarian, liver, and colon cancers.[4] A priority in public health policies, obesity is described as an "epidemic" and a costly burden on healthcare systems. The majority of nutritionists indicate overeating as the main cause for obesity, which nonetheless cannot be decontextualized from environmental factors such as the excessive use of cars and forms of entertainment that do not require physical efforts, as well as the tendency toward overproduction in a market dominated by large food corporations. The global food system produces cheap, calorie-rich, nutrient-poor food and underpays workers, who are then forced to buy cheap food (as many workers in other industries do as well). This vicious cycle keeps the economic system afloat, although in an unsustainable manner, while poorly paid wage earners are ultimately blamed for consuming the wrong kinds of food and therefore for gaining weight.

Accessible and cheap food constantly stimulates us to buy and eat more in a marketplace that is increasingly globalized, competitive, and fragmented. Food advertising and other forms of commercial promotion—from special offers to toys for children—also influence purchasing choices, advancing the food industry's agenda. Yet attempts at curbing overconsumption and establishing sustainable forms of food production and consumption come up against the food industry's ambitions to boost sales constantly to ensure financial returns to their investors.[5] We are relentlessly stimulated to consume more food, and the consequences of such excess are in front of our eyes, both personally and socially.

However, in public discourse, obese people carry the stigma of lack of will and determination. Mainstream popular culture overall denounces large bodies as the consequence of misguided personal choices. Media strive constantly to provide apparently easy solutions to the issue, from piecemeal nutritional advice to diets with doubtful pedigrees. The debates about obesity show how scientific research, medical practices, and nutritional concerns get entangled with cultural bias, social structures, economic interests, and political negotiations. Opinions diverge between considering obesity as a personal matter and framing it as a systemic issue that requires public and political interventions. It's increasingly getting harder for citizens to understand the complexities of public health dynamics that individual decisions simply can't solve in terms of choice and responsibility within a free market.

In this chapter, we'll explore how ideas, values, and practices surrounding a healthy diet are discussed, shaped, and diffused in contemporary postindustrial societies. We'll start from the consumers' experience, focusing on the contradictory advice consumers are exposed to through popular culture and marketing. We'll then reflect on how the industry is trying to take advantage of such confusion to make health claims about its products and how consumers try to ease their anxieties by pinpointing specific ingredients to be avoided.

Against this background, governments try to provide reliable information through *nutritional labels* on packaged food, meant to guide purchasing choices, and food guides, which should offer clear dietary models based on sound nutritional science. However, both tools are enmeshed in political negotiations and are subject to pressures from the food industry lobbying. The chapter will finally explore how the tension between public health and private interests also has an impact on domains as diverse as choices about food in schools and food-safety policies.

Media and Food Fads

What should we do, as consumers and citizens, to take good care of ourselves and our families? What sort of eating habits should we embrace to ensure our health and well-being? We are bombarded with an overwhelming amount of information coming from our peers, media, food producers, national governments, and international organizations. What's worse, the pieces of advice we receive are often contradictory. What sources should we trust? Whose advice is more reliable?

The very nature of scientific research can create a sense of confusion among consumers if not properly explained because its conclusions and recommendations evolve over time by confirming, modifying, or refuting previous findings. Nutrition research is challenging because it is virtually impossible to control the myriad elements that can impact food consumption and behaviors for prolonged periods to isolate and observe specific factors. Human subjects can't be studied like mice. Single-ingredient or single-nutrient studies are particularly difficult. Today salt is bad for you and doctors agree on recommending a reduction in its intake, especially in the presence of heart disease and other chronic conditions. Tomorrow a different report may come out that complicates this clear-cut advice. One day drinking wine is good for you. The next day new studies highlight its dangers. Perplexity caused by nutritional advice is amplified when it's taken out of the context of scientific research and scholarly publications. Furthermore, the influence the food industry wields on researchers by funding studies that usually works in its favor only increases suspicion among the general public.[6] For example, in the 1960s, the sugar industry contributed to studies that minimized the impact of sugar as a risk factor for coronary heart disease while pointing to fat as the main culprit.[7]

In the 1960s, the sugar industry contributed to studies that minimized the impact of sugar as a risk factor for coronary heart disease while pointing to fat as the main culprit.

Media play a central role in maintaining this state of confusion. Media organizations often carry news about health, nutrition, and dieting as concerns about these topics intensify among their audiences. Always looking for exciting stories, writers, bloggers, and newscasters are quick to relay research results without providing any background information. Scientific studies are turned into simple, digestible tips that fit well into forms of communication that favor easy, well-defined explanations of complex topics. Readers are offered bits of unrelated news about this specific nutrient or that substance, without any systematic and thorough explanations. Journalists may opt for clear, simple, ready-to-apply pieces of advice and do-it-yourself recipes, avoiding complex issues and providing a mass of information that often stokes health-related fears. The deluge of piecemeal—at times even contradictory— suggestions from the media gives the impression that science cannot be trusted, with the consequence that consumers may end up heeding the opinions of friends, family, bloggers, influencers, and self-proclaimed experts (often co-opted and paid by special interests and the food industry itself). Exhausted, some decide to just follow their own preferences, arguing that reading one's body is more important than listening to the confusion in the news. Others proceed to "detox" themselves or embark on "full cleanses," supposedly being proactive in taking wellness into their own hands but often subjecting their bodies to unnecessary stress.

Looking for easy-to-follow solutions, consumers end up demonizing certain substances (fat, carbs, gluten) while looking for the next great "superfoods." Products like quinoa, açai, spirulina, goji berries, and moringa constitute a particularly interesting category. They come to the Global North from faraway lands, which increases their exotic charm and allows consumers to attribute them extraordinary nutritional characteristics, often blown out of proportion without the support of serious scientific research. They are sold at high prices, with little or no consideration for the impact that the sudden growth of demand for these products could have on the farmers that grow them, usually located in the Global South. They appeal as comfortable ways out from complicated and potentially stressful choices. Herbal products, traditional remedies, and even references to ancient medical theories, from humors to Ayurveda, provide the same appeasement of anxieties. Such practices are taken out of their cultural and historical context to be packaged and marketed for easy consumption.

Looking for Easy Solutions

Superfoods offer simple—and lucrative—answers to very complex problems: rather than dealing with changes of habits and diets or trying to understand intricate metabolic functions, their consumption assuages the concerns connected with ingestion. The attractiveness of superfoods and exotic or traditional remedies is also related to the diffusion of an approach to eating and health that has been described as *nutritionism*, characterized by "a reductive focus on the nutrient composition of foods as the means for understanding their healthfulness, as well as by a reductive interpretation of the focus of these nutrients in bodily health," with little concern for the level of processing or quality.[8] Consumers attuned to such approaches shift their attention from foods to individual nutrients: polyphenols in red wine are good antioxidants; lycopene in tomatoes can prevent certain kinds of cancer. Such nutrients also can be ingested outside their natural carriers. Why bothering to cook fish when you can simply ingest omega-3 capsules? Why worry about a balanced diet when you can make up for any deficiencies by consuming vitamins, fiber, or fortified foods? Because of the diffusion of such attitudes, which threaten consumers' emotional and cultural connections with food, *nutraceuticals*—a largely unregulated category of dietary supplements that are attributed pharmaceutical-like effectiveness—have become a thriving business.

The food industry takes advantage of such confusion to market its products by touting their allegedly positive contributions to consumers' well-being. Food packaging may carry marketing communication that ranges from health claims ("good for your heart," "lowers your cholesterol") to connections with popular diets ("Atkins-friendly"). Obvious pieces of information try to bank on trends and food fads ("gluten free" on olive oil, for instance), as well as on the addition of supposedly beneficial but unregulated ingredients ("contains activated charcoal"). In some countries, national authorities strictly control such claims and unfounded assertions can be contested in court; elsewhere, the rules are looser, allowing for more creativity on the part of food manufacturers and their marketing departments. Food companies take risks with health claims because they are aware that consumers are receptive, regardless of what nutrition, medicine, biology, and genetics—among other scientific disciplines—indicate as the best advice.

Just as consumers want to be reassured about what is good for them, they also need to identify well-defined culprits they can easily avoid. Public debates, media controversies, and consumers' association campaigns have emerged around substances such as palm oil or high-fructose corn syrup (HFCS), which the food industry routinely adds to prepackaged products to increase their stability and shelf life. Palm oil, traditionally used in West African and Northeastern Brazilian cuisines, is a saturated fat, rich in vitamin A in its fresh form. As the health dangers of trans fats became clear, food manufacturers slowly replaced them with processed palm oil, which shares some of the same properties in terms of food stabilization but may increase risk factors for heart disease. The cultivation of oil palms has expanded from Africa to Malaysia and Indonesia, causing concerns about the environmental impact on forests, which are destroyed to make room for plantations, and on endangered species, such as orangutans in Indonesia. Land may be cleared without the permission of local communities, which become exploited labor in the plantations.

Ethical and health concerns also reverberate in the United States in the controversies surrounding HFCS, a sweetener obtained from cornstarch that is widely used in processing because of its low cost, determined by subsidies for corn production. HFCS, widely present in food of poor nutritional quality, is defended by the industry as a natural product that is not dangerous if consumed in moderation. However, in the public perception it has been tied to the increase in obesity rates and the incidence of heart disease, and it is suspected of retaining contaminants used during its production, such as mercury. The tone of the debate often turns heated, even frenzied, expressing deep-seated anxieties and precluding accurate and careful assessments of the issue.

The cultivation of oil palms has expanded from Africa to Malaysia and Indonesia, causing concerns about the environmental impact on forests, which are destroyed to make room for plantations, and on endangered species, such as orangutans in Indonesia.

Making Sense of Food Labels

Against this background of confusion and misinforma-
tion, governments have recourse to various tools to help
citizens make sound dietary choices and embrace healthy
habits. Nutritional labels on prepackaged food, which governments impose on the food industry, directly communi-
cate with consumers to offer guidance in their purchases.
Labeling regulations are constantly updated to respond
to evolving scientific findings and to improve the clarity
of the information provided to the public. However, the
extent and effectiveness of such updates may vary greatly,
as the food industry constantly pushes back on anything
it perceives as a limitation on their business.

In 2013, Chile introduced logo-like marks to be added
to packaging and containers together with the existing
nutritional labels.[9] Such marks immediately signal when
products are high in calories, sugar, fats, or salt. If these
parameters go beyond specific limits set by law, a product
can be neither advertised to children nor sold in educational establishments. The EU also approved changes in
the regulations concerning labels on prepackaged products in 2014.[10] Beside the existing nutritional information,
products must carry clear indications about the presence
of allergens; mandatory origin information for fresh
meat from pigs, sheep, goats, and poultry; the presence of
added proteins and substitute ingredients for "imitation"

foods; an indication for defrosted products; and a list of any engineered nanomaterials (flavor enhancers, gelation agents, and nanoparticles to remove pathogens from food or to ensure better availability of nutrients are being researched and tested).[11]

Within the EU, various countries are also experimenting with more direct information about the overall health characteristics of prepackaged foods. In 2013, the UK Department of Health introduced a voluntary "traffic light" system in which the content of salt, sugar, fats, and saturated fats is marked as red, amber, or green, according to nutritional guidelines.[12] Foods with a prevalence of reds are to be consumed occasionally or as a treat, whereas those with more greens are to be considered better health choices. The food industry is strongly resisting the system. In 2017, France also adopted a voluntary traffic light model made up of five colors (dark green, light green, yellow, orange, and red), combined with the first five letters of the alphabet, A to E.[13] The letters express the level of wholesomeness (A for most wholesome, E for least), taking into account the favorable characteristics of each product (e.g., the presence of protein, dietary fiber, vitamins, and minerals) in addition to salt, fats, and sugar.

In 2016, the US Food and Drug Administration introduced an updated labeling system it intended to be easier to understand while reflecting the now widely accepted links between diet and chronic diseases.[14] The new labels take a more realistic stance on the serving sizes Americans actually consume (larger than in the past) and make the total number of calories more visible. They also eliminate the number of calories derived from fat, as research suggests that the type of fat consumed is more important than its quantity. Added sugars are clearly marked to avoid excessive consumption; vitamins A and C are no longer indicated because deficiencies are rare; and vitamin D, calcium, iron, and potassium are now signaled. However, these labels immediately caused a strong reaction in the food industry, which constitutes a powerful lobby in the United States. Consequently, the dates for compliance with the new labels have been moved from 2018 to 2020 for manufacturers declaring $10 million or more in food sales per year and to 2021 for those with lower sales.

What Constitutes a Healthful Diet?

The contrast between public health priorities and the financial interests of the food industry (and its investors) also emerges in the negotiations surrounding the development of national dietary guidelines. Based on current nutritional research and meant to direct public health policy and interventions, these guidelines are often very complex and technical. For this reason, governments also issue food guides for the general public that are more accessible and relate to the experience of individuals and their eating choices. Issuing food guides is not a small feat. Within national authorities, contrasting interests and political approaches make deliberations complex and lengthy. Large food businesses, which in many countries wield financial and political influence, also intervene to defend their profits. The result are food guides that often represent compromises among the stakeholders involved.

The United States constitutes an interesting case, as it was one of the first countries to embrace such tools. The US Department of Agriculture (USDA) started publishing food guides in the early 1900s. During World War II, the Guide to Good Eating was issued, defining seven food groups and the optimal quantities of each.[15] The USDA went through several iterations of its recommendations, drawing particular attention with the launch of the Food Guide Pyramid in 1992. This model, reflecting nutrition research and consumers' perceptions, introduced a dietary approach based on concepts of moderation, variety, and proportion among different food groups, clearly indicated by superimposed areas made progressively smaller toward the top to visually indicate what foods need to be consumed in limited quantities.[16] In the following years, the visual pyramid model was also adopted by India and adapted to a pagoda model in China.[17] The United States maintained the pyramid concept in the 2005 MyPyramid Food Guidance System, which underlined the relevance of physical activity by adding "stairs" up the side of the pyramid with a stick figure climbing them and added a new category for oils.[18] However, images of food disappeared and the design changed the food groups from horizontal areas to parallel vertical stripes of different widths, mitigating the visual message that some elements need to be consumed in smaller quantities than others. This idea was reiterated with the launch of MyPlate in 2011, in which a dish is divided into four nearly equivalent areas corresponding to vegetables, fruits, grains, and protein (a nutrient, not a food), accompanied by a small glass that represents dairy.[19]

The plate-based model had already appeared in the United Kingdom with the Eatwell Guide in 2007. In its revision, issued in 2016, the areas dedicated to plant-based foods are visibly larger; moreover, the protein section also includes nuts, beans, and legumes.[20] In 2005 (with revisions in 2010), Japan adopted instead the image of a spinning top, which is basically a pyramid inverted, with dairy and fruit at the bottom and increasingly larger areas moving up for meat and fish dishes, vegetable dishes, and grain dishes.[21] The handle of the top is represented by a glass of water or tea to remind consumers to hydrate properly. A small figure is depicted running on the spinning top, to indicate the centrality of physical activity. The most interesting characteristic here is that the model refers to cooked dishes, rather than ingredients, to make choices easier and more intuitive for consumers. Conceptually similar to the pyramid is the mortar and pestle (*pilon*) chosen to represent good dietary choices in the Dominican Republic. The choice of a kitchen tool that's crucial in many local food preparations is meant to make the representation more appealing to consumers—in particular, to those in the household who choose what to cook and eat.[22]

School Food

Among the measures that governments adopt to improve the diets of their citizens, efforts focusing on school food have multiplied to create healthy food environments for children and to provide nutritious meals by reducing or eliminating excessive fats, sugar, and processed items. (In chapter 6, we'll discuss the relevance of these programs in addressing food insecurity.) In the United States, the National School Lunch Program, in place since 1946, was revised in 2010 with the Healthy, Hunger-Free Kids Act. The regulation required more whole grains, vegetables, and fruits in school meals, reduced sodium and fat intake, and put à la carte menus and vending machines (often a source of high-calorie drinks) under federal control. Such changes were partially rolled back in 2017 when a new administration came to power, demonstrating the relevance of politics and the influence of the food industry on children's nutrition. The importance of national politics also has become evident in Poland, where the government in power since 2015 has softened the previous administration's ban on sales of and ads for junk food—including popular *drożdżówki* sweet buns—on school premises.[23]

Similar initiatives also exist in countries where children struggle to have regular access to food. Since its launch in 1995, the School Lunch Program in India has delivered cooked, balanced meals to millions of primary-school-goers of all castes. Brazil's National School Feeding Program, which provides quality food produced by local farmers and school gardens, offers an example of wide-ranging interventions that are connected with policies aimed at eradicating hunger but also are exposed to changes in the political climate.[24] In 2015, Bolivia launched a law on school food that connects health and food security with food sovereignty (see chapter 7) by giving particular relevance to fresh local crops and ingredients.[25] Such programs frequently draw criticism from political forces that do not believe that governments should meddle with how citizens eat, as well as from those who think that school food constitutes a burden for public finances and taxpayers.

As embattled as they may be, national policies on children's health and nutrition risk missing their goals if they do not include food education, which can take place through dedicated lessons, meals in school cafeterias, gardening, and other food-related activities. Unlike nutrition and health education, which focuses on scientific information about foods that are better to eat and those to avoid, food education introduces children to new ingredients and dishes, their flavors, and their textures, which is not an easy endeavor. It can take several attempts, which can be a financial burden for families with limited incomes that can't afford to throw out new foods that children don't want to eat. As a result, a broad palate and curiosity in tasting new things may become a class marker. To avoid this, each year since 1990 in France, the Week of Taste offers a series of instructional but playful events as part of food education.[26] The initiative is meant to improve children's food behavior and health by educating their *goût* (taste) and familiarizing them with a wide range of foods and flavors—in particular, French culinary traditions.[27] In this case, food education also reflects concerns about the survival of national culinary traditions, perceived as threatened by globalization, and shows political undertones.

Reflecting similar anxieties, in 2005 Japan introduced the Basic Law for Food Education (*shokuiku*) to prevent the abandonment of the Japanese dietary model, considered healthy and nutritious, as a consequence of the growing preference for fast and foreign foods and of changing lifestyles.[28] In 2008, the international Slow Food association launched the Edible School Gardens initiative, geared toward sensory education, as well as instruction about environmental, food production, and local food cultures.[29] It follows the example of chef Alice Waters, who started the Edible Schoolyard project in the late 1990s in California to introduce children to healthy eating and different vegetable varieties.[30] Chefs also are getting involved. TV celebrity Jamie Oliver launched a "food revolution" in the United Kingdom through a show that aired in 2005 and showed the dismal state of school food in the country. The public reaction was so intense that the government invested sizeable funds into improving the situation, with mixed results.[31]

Managing Risk and Food Safety

The tension between the interests of the food industry and the well-being of citizens is apparent when it comes to food safety, a central concern for governments with major political implications, as we discussed in the previous chapter. In 1986, twenty-three people died in Italy for ingesting methanol that had been added to wine illegally to raise its alcohol content. In 1996, the EU voted for a total ban on beef from the United Kingdom because of the diffusion of bovine spongiform encephalopathy (BSE, more commonly known as *mad cow disease*). In 2008, milk and infant formula in China were adulterated with melamine, causing a hundred thousand illnesses and a few deaths and prompting the national authorities to decree executions and life prison for individuals involved, including officials. In the same year, over seven hundred people fell ill from salmonella in the United States after eating peanut butter from the Peanut Corporation of America, triggering the most extensive food recall to date. In 2011, an outbreak of over 1,500 cases of *E. coli* in Germany and other European countries, many of which presented life-threatening complications, was blamed on organic cucumbers grown in Southern Spain; the outbreak damaged consumers' trust in organic products. In 2017, consumption of processed meat caused one of the world's worst listeria outbreaks in South Africa, with almost two hundred victims. These and other innumerable—and luckily less deadly—cases have changed perceptions about food-related risks and food-safety practices around the world.

National authorities embrace different approaches to the protection of consumers: some leave it to food producers to self-regulate, while others impose strict controls and procedures. A few countries are gearing up to mandate *traceability*—the possibility of tracing a product back through all stages of production, processing, distribution, and retail while identifying all actors involved—as a measure to organize quick recalls in case of emergencies such as salmonella outbreaks or food contamination. Ongoing conflicts can be observed between the need for public interventions and coordination among all stakeholders in the food system on the one hand and the desire of authorities to avoid burdening entrepreneurs and businesses with excessive regulations on the other. To address such tensions at the international level, since 1961 the Food and Agriculture Organization of the United Nations (FAO) and the World Health Organization published the *Codex Alimentarius*, a constantly updated and internationally accepted set of standards, guidelines, and recommendations to ensure food safety and safeguard consumers' health.[32] Furthermore, the World Trade Organization introduced the Agreement on Sanitary and Phytosanitary Measures (the SPS Agreement), concerning the application of food-safety regulations in international trade.

Behavioral changes in dietary habits, better nutrition, and food safety—although crucial—are not the only aspects that require public action at the national and international levels to contribute to individual and communal health. In the next chapter, we'll discuss how food systems also need to prioritize the well-being of all stakeholders involved by embracing the ambitious goal of long-term sustainability from environmental, social, and economic points of view.

ENVIRONMENT AND SUSTAINABILITY

How many times have you opened the fridge to find molding cheese, wilting lettuce, leftovers you forgot about, or eggs too old to use? You can easily throw these items away to make room for the next trip to the grocery store or to the market or to wherever you buy food. This stuff isn't that expensive, so it's not a big deal to get rid of it. It's all so normal that we may not give a second thought to the fact that we own a fridge, that we have food to store in it, and that access to more food is relatively easy and cheap. But this is quite a feat, one that isn't even imaginable for so many other individuals and families around the world. Beyond the obvious privilege, we may not realize that we're entangled in a larger problem that's haunting the global food system, not only in the Global North but also in less developed areas: food waste.

The waste of food that is left uneaten, discarded because it's spoiled, or lost in the supply network because of inefficiencies in production and distribution offers a particularly interesting entry point to start examining issues of sustainability in the food system. *Sustainability* refers to approaches that balance the use of resources in the present with their long-term availability in the future. Although food waste is just one aspect that needs to be dealt with to address sustainability, we experience it tangibly on the one hand, especially in terms of the money we lose and the guilt we may (or may not) experience. On the other hand, we are discarding not only individual items but also all the resources, energy, and inputs that go into producing them. Preventing waste means more than just shopping smarter and making sure that we use everything we buy. It requires dealing with problems that plague our global food system and need to be tackled in their totality and in their complex interconnections. Starting from uneaten and discarded food, this chapter will examine the environmental features that affect sustainability in the food system (waste management, water and air pollution, soil degradation, deforestation, conservation, energy, greenhouse gas emissions), as well as their social and economic aspects (human health, justice and equality, labor exploitation, accessibility, efficiency). All these elements need to be observed within the broader framework of our time's most critical emergency, climate change, which already

The waste of food that is left uneaten, discarded because it's spoiled, or lost in the supply network because of inefficiencies in production and distribution offers a particularly interesting entry point to start examining issues of sustainability in the food system.

has an impact on what we grow and how we grow it. Not only does climate change affect food production, but food production itself also contributes to climate change.

Food Waste

Measuring food waste is not easy, and debates have developed on the methods used to gather and analyze data.[1] The FAO estimated that in 2007 about 1.6 billion tons out of a total of six billion tons of food produced went to waste globally, creating a carbon footprint equivalent to 7 percent of all global emissions.[2] A recent study found that US consumers on average waste about a pound of food (30 percent of daily calories available) every day. Such food is grown on thirty million acres of cropland every year, equivalent to 7 percent of annual cropland acreage.[3]

The roots of the issue go well beyond the lack of planning or the carelessness of consumers. Waste is embedded in supply networks, starting from agricultural fields and other production sites. These dynamics are particularly urgent in developing countries, where the lack of adequate infrastructures, investment, farmers' education, and technical personnel is glaring. Waste may occur in countless ways. Lack of coordination may prevent parts of crops from being collected. Prices may drop so low that farmers would lose money if they invested funds in harvesting.

Products may be exposed to weather or pests during transportation or warehousing, or farmers may not have sufficient connections to markets. Produce that doesn't meet the quality standards–sometimes including aesthetic requirements—imposed by small and large buyers is often discarded. Milk may go to waste because of poor refrigeration during collection or scarce hygiene in dairy plants. Further losses happen during distribution, storage, and sales. Defective packaging also can be a culprit.

Supply networks in the Global North are not immune from food waste. Overproduction may push authorities to impose quotas and destroy crops and products to keep prices at levels that ensure acceptable revenues to producers. EU citizens are routinely angered by the destruction of milk, tomatoes, and oranges, among other products, which seem particularly offensive when many fellow citizens do not have enough to eat. Consumers may not want to buy fruits and vegetables that do not look perfect, with the consequence that unsold produce may be thrown out even though it's perfectly edible. Shoppers may be confused by "use by," "best before," and other information on packaging, refusing to purchase food that is still safe. Stores, supermarkets, restaurants, schools, hospitals, army messes, and cafeterias may throw out unused food. In fact, they may not be allowed to store cooked food for consumption at a later time or for distribution to charities because of safety regulations.

Such breathtaking waste has generated practices that manage to take advantage of it. Underprivileged populations in large urban centers that do not have other opportunities to feed themselves routinely search for usable materials and food in landfills. Gleaners roam fields to gather whatever is left after the harvest. At times, reactions may have political undertones. Dumpster divers salvage discarded food items from garbage containers as well. Freegans avoid engaging with the monetary economy and embrace alternative strategies, such as squatting and "guerilla gardening" in city parks or abandoned spaces.

Social discomfort with food waste, inefficient but also unethical and unsustainable, is stimulating efforts to limit it at all levels of supply networks. Organic waste can be composted into fertilizer to improve agricultural yields or "digested" in technological plants to generate biogas that can be refined and used as fuel or converted into electricity. Food oils are recycled into biodiesels to replace fossil fuels, creating a market for the acquisition and use of used frying oils from fast foods and restaurants. Start-ups are finding new ways to turn leftovers from food manufacturing into inputs for food and nonfood products: old bread is fermented into beer, and used barley from beer brewing is ground into baking flour. Orange peels from juice factories become textiles, and grape leftovers from winemaking are processed into faux leather. "Ugly" or damaged fruit can be squeezed into juices, turned into jams and sorbets, or dried and powdered to add flavor to seasoning mixes. Chefs are rethinking menus to limit food waste and use all edible parts of ingredients. Innovative packaging materials change color when the content turns bad, helping consumers avoid throwing out food that is still good. Software using demand-modeling algorithms can generate reliable projections by factoring in demand variability, can improve logistics, and can reduce waste by fine-tuning on-time transportation and communication among the actors in a supply network. Such technologies are particularly effective for perishable goods such as fresh fish, vegetables, and fruits. Apps allow restaurants and stores to send information about unused food to charities and other organizations that can make good use of it.

Creativity and innovation definitely contribute to mitigating the effects of food waste that are visible to consumers—and thus are perceived as socially and politically relevant. However, to deal effectively with the issue, it's necessary to concentrate efforts on the complex relationships among the environment, production, and society at large. Beyond optimizing the manufacturing and life cycle of a single product, already a relevant and worthy endeavor, the next step is to examine the flow of energy and materials across supply networks. Such complexity demands a change of mentality and a shift toward systemic perspectives. Food is connected to water, energy, and other inputs that require infrastructures, transportation, and other technologies, which in turn entail broader environmental and industrial policies. Climate change, the most urgent challenge that connects all these issues at a global level, needs intensive international cooperation beyond the involvement of national governments, local communities, small and large businesses, producers in all sectors, and consumers. However, as all these stakeholders address the issue with different values, goals, and priorities, any decision about climate change turns into a political challenge.

These tensions also intensify because sustainability cannot refer to environmental protection and resource conservation only, but also needs to include long-term economic viability and social equity. As this implies addressing causes rather than just mitigating consequences, such an approach requires public policy interventions, as well as changes in corporate decision-making processes.[4] These dynamics indicate that the very concept of sustainability is predicated on a collective perspective because it indicates forms of growth and development that embrace limitations on today's consumption to ensure the ability of future generations to meet their own needs.

Assessing Agricultural Practices

Considering sustainability as a priority while ensuring enough food for the growing global population leads to reevaluating the epochal transformations that have been taking place in food production. Mechanization, intensification, and logistic innovations (see chapter 2) have enormously increased agricultural yields and the availability of affordable food worldwide. However, the focus on increasing production through technology came at a price, at times causing the loss of small farms and the devastation of rural communities. The expansion of agriculture to areas that were not particularly fertile required massive irrigation, the intensification of cultivation, and the search for increasingly higher yields. These changes took place together with a staggering upsurge in the use of chemicals, from fertilizers to pesticides and herbicides. Such dynamics were exported to developing countries starting in the late 1960s under the name of the green revolution (see chapter 5).

In the nineteenth century, the traditional use of manure from local farm animals had already been replaced by more efficient sources of nitrogen to replenish the soil—in particular, guano, the excrement of seabirds and bats accumulated in great quantities on islands off the coast of Peru, as well as in the Caribbean and elsewhere. Due to its remarkably elevated content of nitrogen, phosphate, and potassium, guano constituted such an important resource despite the costs of collecting and transporting it that disputes for its control turned at times into wars. However, its relevance waned after the Haber-Bosch process of industrial nitrogen fixation was invented in the early 1900s to produce ammonia-based fertilizers (ironically, the same technology was also used to develop chemical weapons). New arsenic pesticides and DDT were introduced, replaced over time by organophosphates, pyrethrin, and triazine, among others. In fact, DDT was proven to be hazardous for humans and to affect the reproduction rates of some bird species. The environmental movements that developed worldwide in the 1960s and 1970s, fueled by books like Rachel Carson's *Silent Spring*, published in 1962, led to the introduction of legislation that reined in the indiscriminate use of synthetic pesticides.

Environmental issues connected with agriculture are far from being resolved. Fertilizers and pesticides can be washed away easily by rain. They infiltrate water reserves, pollute rivers, and run off to the oceans, damaging wildlife and stimulating the excessive growth of algae and microorganisms. These residues can suffocate whole ecological systems. In the Gulf of Mexico, runoff from agricultural areas in the Midwest has created a dead zone in which lack of oxygen due to algal growth is destroying marine life—and this zone is as large as the country of Belize.[5] New genetically modified crops are now available that are resistant to specific pesticides, like glyphosate, making spraying innocuous for those plants. However, the pesticides' effects on consumers are hotly debated because chemical residues can be harmful to humans. It isn't unusual for

In the Gulf of Mexico, runoff from agricultural areas in the Midwest has created a dead zone in which lack of oxygen due to algal growth is destroying marine life— and this zone is as large as the country of Belize.

chemicals to be sprayed while workers are on the fields; they may be unable to protest because they're undocumented, afraid of losing their jobs, or lacking in political clout.[6] Chemical inputs are also widely employed in small farms all around the world, where workers may not be properly trained to use them correctly. The success of *organic agriculture* is partly a reaction to these concerns. Animal species also can be threatened by artificial agricultural inputs: nicotine-based pesticides seem to be harmful to bees, despite agribusinesses' claims to the contrary. The global decrease of the bee population is causing concern because bees are the main pollinators for many crops. A market for traveling beehives that are temporarily located where needed has developed to respond to this emergency. These kinds of Band-Aid interventions, however, do not address the global decline of pollinators, a major risk for agriculture.

The worldwide diffusion of mechanization, which cuts labor costs and expedites harvesting, has led to a preference for high-yield varieties cultivated in monoculture conditions, which also respond to the needs of the meat industry's growing demand for animal feed. Soy and corn have become among the most widely cultivated crops worldwide, but only very limited varieties are used. The expansion of monocultures has streamlined crop production from sowing to growing, collecting, and transporting. It has also caused heavy losses in terms of biodiversity:

varieties that provide lower yields or require more manual labor are abandoned. However, a wider assortment of varieties of the same species, each with its own characteristics and strengths, can constitute a form of insurance against the diffusion of pests and diseases, which can have devastating effects if cultivations only include a single variety susceptible to these issues. Richer agrobiodiversity also ensures a greater availability of species that may better adapt to soil salinization, erosion, and depletion, as well as the consequences of changing climate conditions, droughts, and floods. In Mexico, traditional corn varieties frequently have been replaced with more "modern" seeds that are supposed to have higher yields. However, the old varieties had been selected by generations of farmers to adapt to specific natural environments and soils, ensuring a sufficient harvest during dry spells in which the new varieties are not able to grow as expected.

Monocultures also affect the complex ecologies that have evolved around specific species. Coffee is a well-known case. Instead of growing under a shade canopy of mixed native trees that provide a habitat for migrating birds, coffee plants are cultivated in wide, open fields that, in addition to requiring the destruction of wide swaths of rainforest, leave little room for other plant species and for birds that control insect pests and pollinate crops. The production of so-called shade-grown coffee is now supported by organizations that aim to protect both the forest environment and the animals that live in them.

The Impact of Animal and Fish Farming

The application of industrial methods to achieve economies of scale is not limited to agriculture. Meat production operations have adopted similar models, which better respond to the growth in demand both in the Global North and in developing countries. The conversion of forest to cattle pasture is among the main causes of deforestation in countries such as Brazil, Colombia, and Costa Rica. *Concentrated animal-feeding operations* (CAFOs), in which beef cattle, dairy cows, pigs, or chickens are raised in extremely confined spaces, are increasingly common. They have become quite controversial because they tend to physically displace or to push out of business smaller enterprises that may instead favor less constricted spaces for poultry and livestock. The proximity of animals in CAFOs requires the administration of antibiotics to avoid bacterial infections, but the presence of such substances in meat can contribute to the rise of antibiotic-resistant "superbugs" that can't be eliminated with traditional treatments. Livestock operations also sometimes employ hormones that accelerate the growth of their animals but may have negative effects on consumers' health. As concerns about antibiotics and hormones grow among consumers, many agribusinesses are taking measures to limit or eliminate their use.

Livestock raised in CAFOs tend to be slaughtered in mechanized plants that constitute environmental hazards in themselves and a threat to food safety if the meat is not properly treated. To keep labor costs low, these businesses at times employ undocumented workers, whose personal safety can be jeopardized by the fast rhythms of production and the use of dangerous machinery. Furthermore, the lack of labor protection and controls can lead to exploitation and sexual harassment. CAFOs may also have adverse consequences on the environment. The huge amount of gases such as methane and ammonia emitted by dense concentrations of animals negatively affects air quality and makes living nearby difficult to bear. Added emissions derive from the fossil fuels used to sow, fertilize, and harvest animal feed, which also diverts land and water from the production of crops for human consumption. Open lagoons in which waste flows to be treated attract insects and other vermin. CAFOs are sometimes built in the vicinities of disadvantaged communities that have little social and political negotiating power to oppose them; members of these communities find themselves stuck in place as the real estate values of their homes plummet. CAFOs also use vast amounts of water to raise animals and keep them clean. If waste and manure aren't properly treated, dangerous substances, pathogens, and antibiotics can spill over and contaminate both groundwater and surface water in the surrounding areas, ending up in rivers, lakes, and eventually oceans.

Open waters are threatened by the expansion of fish farming as well. Consumers are increasingly more aware of the benefits of fish protein, which comes with little saturated fat and plenty of polyunsaturated fats, such as omega-3 and omega-6 fatty acids. The demand for seafood has increased, supported by improved transportation and conservation technologies. As a consequence, overfishing has decimated wild fisheries. This is an example of the "tragedy of the commons:" individual actors—mostly fishing corporations—race to take advantage of a scarce shared resource in the hopes of making a short-term profit before the resource disappears, regardless of the common good of the community. Luckily, alternative experiences exist in which shared resources are collectively managed through cooperatives that are governed by the users themselves.[7] Regulations have been adopted at the national and international levels, imposing measures to limit fishing and replenish the wild fisheries, with partial success. Educational campaigns have focused on explaining seafood sustainability to shoppers, indicating which fish are in danger of extinction or are part of unsound supply networks. Consumers are also encouraged to eat lower on the food chain by opting for squid, mollusks, shrimp, and small fish like anchovies, sardines, and herring. Chefs and culinary professionals are looking at ways to make *trash fish*, species that aren't usually eaten, more interesting and appealing.

Although intensive fish farming in both sweet waters and the oceans fills the gap in seafood demand, concerns have been voiced about these practices. Carnivore species require fish feed, partly composed of small wild-caught fish, which exacerbates overfishing: several pounds of wild fish, which could also be directed to human consumption, are used for every pound of farmed salmon. Fish are raised in high concentrations, which increases the risk for disease and parasites to spread and pushes operators to use antibiotics that can eventually enter the environment. As in the case of meat, the presence of antibiotics raises health concerns for consumers, who are often doubtful about the overall quality of farmed seafood. Fragile habitats like mangrove swamps have been destroyed to build fish farms in nations such as Thailand, India, Ecuador, and Costa Rica. The presence of fish farms, especially if concentrated in a small area, can have a negative impact on the surrounding environment because waste can easily get dispersed in the water. In Vietnam, rice paddies have been turned into lucrative shrimp farms, but when an excess of medicinal substances and polluted matter makes the ponds useless, the soil is too contaminated to be repurposed for rice cultivation, an activity that is otherwise culturally and socially central to the traditional livelihood in rural regions.

Ecological damage can occur if nonnative species are unintentionally introduced into the wild. Genetically modified fish are being engineered with traits that ensure faster growth and resistance to the artificial conditions of fish farms. The possibility of such species finding their way into the open has generated anxiety among not only environmentalists but also large segments of consumers that look at GMOs with suspicion. However, seafood farming also can be beneficial when practiced correctly. Raising oysters in cages, for instance, can be sustainable: the oysters filter phytoplankton and excessive nutrients out of the water, while their waste provides nourishment to microorganisms that are consumed in turn by crabs and other sea creatures. Moreover, oyster beds are also being studied as a possible means to counteract the loss of the wetland habitats that used to mitigate coastal flooding.

The Greatest Challenge: Climate Change

The expansion of industrialized agriculture, as well increases in meat and seafood production, have crucial consequences for the health and dietary patterns of consumers, the labor conditions of farmers and workers, and the sustainable use of land, water, and other resources.

Raising oysters in cages ... can be sustainable: the oysters filter phytoplankton and excessive nutrients out of the water, while their waste provides nourishment to microorganisms that are consumed in turn by crabs and other sea creatures.

Research suggests the changing conditions of food production have a direct impact on the global phenomenon of climate change. Although the dynamics of this connection are complex and multilayered, the main drivers have been identified: deforestation, energy use in agriculture, and methane and other gases generated by livestock farming.

Through photosynthesis, plants use carbon dioxide (CO_2) to grow. Nevertheless, research indicates that an excess of the gas can compromise the presence of protein, zinc, and iron in edible crops.[8] CO_2 is among the gases that absorb and emit heat within the thermal infrared range, contributing to the greenhouse effect and raising temperatures around the planet. While the expansion of cultivated crops increases the amount of CO_2 captured in vegetation, deforestation to make more land available for agriculture releases large amounts of CO_2 into the atmosphere, adding to the emissions from the combustion of fossil fuels. The expansion in the production of *biofuels* from plants, often supported by government subsidies as a sustainable addition to nonrenewable fossil fuels, also has an impact on greenhouse emissions. On the one hand, the CO_2 absorbed by the plants from which biofuels derive may offset the CO_2 emissions generated when they're used as fuel. On the other hand, when additional land is cleared to grow crops for biofuels, CO_2 is released into the atmosphere. Whether the overall impact is positive or negative is under debate. Furthermore, energy and fuels are needed for the cultivation of these plants and their transformation into biofuels. As more agricultural land shifts to biofuel production, the prices of edible crops may increase, stimulating farmers to clear more land and causing additional releases of CO_2. Such an effect can be mitigated by the production of ethanol from algae, fungi, and nonedible plants such as jatropha, or by using cellulose byproducts from food production, like sugarcane leftovers from sugar manufacturing. Food production—in particular, livestock farming—generates the emission of other gases beside CO_2, such as methane and nitrous oxide, which also contribute to the greenhouse effect, one of the main causes of climate change. Moreover, shifts in land use, with their consequent alterations to the distribution of vegetation, influence the reflection of light and heat off the planet's surface, contributing to a rise in temperatures.

The introduction of new high-yield varieties and technologies, together with the expansion of cultivated land, requires massive irrigation. Today, agriculture counts for 70 percent of the global use of fresh water.[9] Drinking water has become a luxury in many areas of the world. Shifting irrigation patterns are likely to affect humidity and cloud circulation in the atmosphere, altering rainfall distribution and indirectly worsening the greenhouse effect. Moreover, irrigation has become a major contributor to water scarcity and the depletion of aquifers around the world. Both small rural enterprises and large agrobusinesses invest in drilling and wells, even if the temporary advantages connected with more water availability are likely to cause long-term problems. Instead of fighting for water conservation in the public interest, governments often adopt policies that reflect the interests of the agricultural sector. For many smallholders, water availability can literally make the difference between life and death. Studies are underway on the optimization of water use through improved crop distribution and more efficient irrigation, while avoiding land use change to extend crop cultivation.[10] However, larger corporations usually are better positioned to take advantage of available resources, at the expense of less powerful stakeholders, contributing to vicious circles of inequality.

Climate change could potentially generate benefits, such as greater precipitation, higher temperatures, and longer growing seasons, in areas that were previously too arid and too cold for agriculture. Farmers in upstate New York state now enjoy a longer growing season and the possibility of cultivating more diverse crops. A whole new wine industry is developing in countries such as Poland and Denmark thanks to both the development of grape hybrids adapted to cold environments and a warmer climate. However, such increases in localized productivity are unlikely to make up for the negative consequences of climate change on global agriculture, affected by the irregularity of weather patterns, more frequent droughts, sudden and violent floods, and the overall greater intensity of meteorological events.[11] In addition to causing heat stress for crops, higher temperatures favor the proliferation of pests, alter soil geochemistry, and cause possible shocks to soil microbiotas that are crucial for the healthy growth of plants. Higher temperatures also can accelerate growth processes and increase irrigation water evaporation, to the detriment of plants' health.

Embracing New Perspectives

Food geographies are shifting globally, forcing production patterns and economies to adjust and reorganize themselves. As the interconnection between agriculture and climate change becomes clearer, new resilience, adaptation, and mitigation strategies are required that move away from the exclusive focus on increasing production. Offering a diverging path from the green revolution approach, which favored mechanization and intensive use of inputs (see chapter 5), emerging agroecological methods emphasize agrobiodiversity, synergies among different production sectors, composting and repurposing of materials, and a more efficient use of resources and inputs. They also incorporate local crops that farming communities around the world have developed over generations, as well as traditional technologies for soil management.

Crops that had been almost abandoned because of their low yields, high labor requirements, or scarce adaptability to industrial production methods are newly appreciated because of their resiliency, resistance to drought, and nutritional value. For example, the cultivation of fonio, a tiny grain originally from the Sahel area in sub-Saharan Africa, is expanding thanks both to the plant's capacity to tolerate drought conditions and to its lack of gluten, which meets consumers' evolving preferences in the Global North. In East Africa, farmers have reintroduced sorghum, millets, and various beans to counteract the failure of rains. In India, traditional rice varieties, green gram, and many pulses are being embraced as a response to water scarcity. The same is happening in Central America with amaranth.

Seed companies and biotech labs also are participating in the research on drought-tolerant crops, both through traditional selection processes and genetic modification. However, in the case of GMOs, the agribusiness's ownership of the intellectual property of genetic materials limits farmers' control over their crops because seeds from one year's harvest legally can't be set aside and used in the following growing seasons (see chapter 5).

Daring initiatives and new perspectives are necessary to address long-term sustainability in ways that take into consideration environmental, economic, and social issues while responding to consumers' needs and preferences. Not only food producers but also all other stakeholders in the global food system have to be involved, including celebrity chefs. US chef Dan Barber, for instance, has suggested that farmers shouldn't grow what consumers (including chefs) demand, but instead we should all consume what the farmers need to grow to maintain the fertility of their soil and the viability of farming as a productive activity. Italian chef Massimo Bottura has launched soup kitchens where famous chefs cook food that otherwise would go to waste to feed those in need. Brazilian chef Alex Atala has highlighted plants and animals from the Amazon to provide jobs to people from the area and support better environmental management. Senegalese chef Pierre Thiam promotes fonio around the world, opening markets for smallholders in the Sahel area.

Although consumers, activists, and producers certainly play a central role in ushering innovation in the food system, the intervention of institutions, governments, researchers, and policymakers—both at the national and international levels—is fundamental to tackle urgent global issues that no single stakeholder can address, such as climate change. Solutions have to be found at a systemic level that include changes in consumption patterns, waste prevention, infrastructure improvements, efficient management of renewable resources, sustainable practices in food production, and advanced ecological approaches. The relevance of scientists, engineers, and designers operating in these domains cannot be discounted. Although not a silver bullet, technology need not necessarily be considered the enemy of sustainability, a position often embraced by those who fight for a healthier, fairer, and more environmentally friendly food system. Everything depends on who sets the agenda and the priorities for research, who owns the resulting technology, who has access to it and how, and its uses. As we'll discuss in the next chapter, if managed through democratic means and not used only to concentrate power and wealth in the hands of a few, technology can play a positive role. It can introduce innovation, support change, and offer viable solutions for urgent problems in the global food system.

TECHNOLOGY

As we discussed in the previous chapters, the global food system is in need of serious changes. However, the recipes for solutions that have been emerging diverge greatly, pointing to very different concerns and interpretations of the current situations. Are we all going to starve, as Malthus prophesized in the eighteenth century? Or will we always find ways to feed humankind, regardless of its expansion, thanks to scientific advancements, technologies, and resourcefulness? What transformations should take place for us to be resilient, reacting and adapting to the consequences of climate change? Will they be based on intensive industrial agriculture, on the rediscovery and adaptation of our ancestors' ways, on the application of evolving scientific research on ecology and sustainability, or on solutions that draw from all these approaches? Each response is far from being objective and neutral: it is rather the expression of ideologies and political negotiations that are solidly rooted in our present and in our evaluation of the societies we live in.[1]

This chapter will focus on how the growing role of technology in the global food system both eases and amplifies concerns about what, why, and how we eat now and what the future holds. In particular, we'll explore the ownership of intellectual property, the role and scope of innovation in food production, and the relationships of consumers with technological change in their daily lives. To examine these issues, we first need to look at how the contributions—or the threats—of technology and science to the food system are understood and dealt with in practice. The evaluation of the risks and benefits of technology depends on who is doing the assessment, their position in the food system, and what kind of negative or positive impact they could experience.

Utopias and Dystopias

In political, media, and civil society debates about the introduction of technology, visions for the future emerge on a continuum between utopia and dystopia, with humankind's ingenuity and creativity always producing new, positive solutions on one end and nightmarish scenarios, in which science and technology become tools of oppression and destruction or rebel against their own creators, on the other end. Of course, certain utopic approaches disavow technology completely and do not even consider its potential. We can recognize such positions in the Luddites in England, who in the early nineteenth century saw the destruction of machines as the only viable opposition to exploitation, and in the 1960s and 1970s back-to-the-land movement in the United States, in which emphasis was given to physical work, self-reliance, and manual production of goods to escape the strictures of capitalist society. The utopian points of view that embrace technology instead express the stance that the food system can only gain from the introduction of innovations ranging from laboratory experimentations on GMOs to replacement meats. This kind of future has constituted a boundless frontier for the imagination in popular culture: Will we feed ourselves with pills that contain all the nutrients we need? Will we be able to construct food out of thin air, assembling atoms floating in the environment, like in *The Jetsons*? Will small, dehydrated lumps turn into full-on roast chicken meals, like in Luc Besson's 1997 film, *The Fifth Element*? Or will we instead be forced to consume deceased humans in the form of protein bars, like in Richard Fleischer's 1973 film, *Soylent Green*?

The culinary arts have been at the forefront of the explorations of what and how we eat, and above all how to cook, generating stimulating ideas for chefs, researchers,

Will we be able to construct food out of thin air, assembling atoms floating in the environment, like in *The Jetsons*? Will small, dehydrated lumps turn into full-on roast chicken meals, like in … *The Fifth Element*? Or will we instead be forced to consume deceased humans in the form of protein bars, like in … *Soylent Green*?

food scientists, and food enthusiasts. New techniques such as foam making and sous vide cooking have spread quickly, while research in the chemical and physical characteristics of ingredients have spurred the use of liquid nitrogen, alginates, and collagens in the kitchen.[2] *Molecular gastronomy* (which studies the physical and chemical changes food undergoes when cooked) and *neurogastronomy* (focusing on how the brain processes flavors, smells, and textures) are among the fields of research that have emerged from innovative interactions among culinary arts, sciences, and technology.[3] Such approaches, however, do not claim to offer contributions to the larger issues haunting the food system.

Reliance on and even delight in technology can provoke visceral reactions that take the shape of dystopian visions, as justified fears exist that mass-manufacturing, mechanization, and the intensive use of food-science research will lead to a total dehumanization of the food system and increased risks for human health and the environment. Technology is identified as a cause for the exclusion of whole segments of the human population from crucial decisions about what we grow and consume. Within this camp, forms of opposition to the current food system are emerging that support human-centered production models. In the culinary world, chefs are embracing farm-to-table dining; they highlight the provenance of their ingredients—emphasizing local and organic ones in particular—and stress the skill in their craft. The nutritional features, the origin, and the cultural value of what we eat are increasingly relevant for growing segments of consumers in the Global North. Such approaches, while placing health and sustainability at their core, can veer toward nostalgia for traditional and artisanal foods and express indifference—if not open mistrust—toward innovation. Embraced by numerous proponents of the *food movement* that aims to change the global food system for the better, these attitudes have been at times dubbed *culinary luddism* because they may fail to acknowledge the contribution of modernization to food security in the forms of abundant, durable, accessible, and affordable products.[4] The interventions they favor have been criticized as elitist and ineffective in tackling the enormous scale of the food system and its problems.

The utopian perspective considers technological globalization inevitable at worst and an advantage at best, criticizing opposing perspectives as pastoral nostalgias. The dystopian outlook, meanwhile, decries excessive reliance on technology as a scourge unleashed all around the world by political and technocratic choices that can be opposed—or at least mitigated, by embracing the local dimension as the gold standard. However, the dichotomy between tradition and modernity, artisanal skills and technology does not hold. Ancient agricultural methods can support contemporary ecological approaches to food production, while newfangled tools in food science may support dying artisanal traditions, improving food quality, safety, and durability. Change has been integral to the food system since its inception at the beginning of the agricultural revolution, thousands of years ago. It doesn't pay to demonize technology, lest we risk forgetting that even a spoon is a piece of technology—and an evolving one at that. The interaction of science and creativity can generate new opportunities in all aspects of the food system. Technology has the potential to improve agricultural productivity, resilience to climate change, and the environmental impact of crop cultivations, livestock farming, and fisheries. Innovative instruments can be applied to develop vertical farming, sustainable fisheries, and humane animal pens.

What really counts is who controls the research agenda, whose interests and priorities the research reflects, and who owns the intellectual property tied to the discoveries that derive from it. We always need to consider how technology spreads, who has the financial power to invest in it and implement it, and whether it favors or hinders the democratic participation of all stakeholders involved.

Who Owns Technology? The GMO Case

Assessments of the social impact of new technologies in terms of who has access to them and who gains from them

Ancient agricultural methods can support contemporary ecological approaches to food production, while newfangled tools in food science may support dying artisanal traditions. ... It doesn't pay to demonize technology, lest we risk forgetting that even a spoon is a piece of technology—and an evolving one at that.

are crucial, but they have not always been at the forefront of rural development agendas. Echoing the growing fears that there would not be enough food for a growing human population, the 1960s and 1970s saw intense top-down efforts to introduce technologies and management methods in agriculture as part of the *green revolution*. The term was coined in 1968 by William Gaud, director of the US Agency for International Development, to denote a set of measures aimed at increasing agricultural output by introducing high-yield crop varieties, often grown in monoculture with the support of fertilizers, pesticides, irrigation, and mechanization. The Rockefeller Foundation and the Ford Foundation, international organizations like the FAO, and the United States, which provided economic aid and could use its political weight, promoted these interventions among governments in the developing world. The green revolution saw its first concrete application with the introduction of wheat varieties in Mexico right after World War II, which turned the country into a wheat exporter within twenty years. This new agricultural approach soon was applied in many Southeast Asian countries and India, which also implemented ambitious measures such as the systematic exploitation of groundwater resources, the adoption of new land-management techniques, and electrification.[5] Indonesia planted new rice varieties, the selection of which had started in laboratories in the Philippines in the early 1960s. The government made major investments into creating the scientific infrastructure that was necessary to adapt these varieties to local environments. It also launched the extension services and farming cooperatives necessary to spread the new technologies among farmers, while building a rural banking system and a bureaucracy able to manage the effort. Rice production tripled over about thirty years, allowing Indonesia to achieve self-sufficiency and to start exporting. However, most efforts focused on land that was already the most productive, like the island of Java. Over time, the focus on the production intensification of a few varieties had a negative impact on biodiversity and increased the vulnerability of harvests. A single infestation could wipe out whole crops, as happened in the mid-1970s with the outbreak of the so-called brown plant hopper. The new technologies saw an increase in the use of chemical inputs that was not strictly necessary but was supported by local policies. When the subsidies for pesticides were stopped in the early 1990s, farmers immediately started applying less of them, without major consequences. The innovation also involved profound cultural changes; segments of populations in Bali, for example, resisted the new methods because they impinged on *subak*, the traditional management of irrigated paddy fields.

Attempts to introduce the green revolution in Africa were less successful than those in Asia, due to factors such as corruption and inefficiency in local and national governments, lack of infrastructure, and specific environmental issues like water scarcity and soil fragility. The green revolution, hailed by many as a success, particularly in terms of yields, often proved to be unsustainable in the long term from an environmental point of view, causing a loss of biodiversity, water overuse, soil impoverishment, pollution related to herbicides and fertilizers, and increased use of fossil fuels to operate machinery.[6] Moreover, the direct involvement of transnational agribusiness corporations and their research and development departments guaranteed dominant positions for the holders of intellectual property tied to seeds and other technological inputs.

The most glaring examples of the social and political relevance of ownership of technology are found in cases tied to genetically modified (GM) crops, in which genes are transferred among varieties of the same species and across species without sexual crossing, as was the case in traditional methods of hybridization and selection. So far, public debates have mostly focused on the risks the introduction of GM organisms may generate for human health and the environment. However, more studies and clinical trials are required, and research has not reached conclusive results yet.[7] Less attention has been paid to who retains the legal rights to the use of technology, what model of agriculture it fosters, how it is introduced, and what kind of crops or animals are targeted for research and development.

The historical turning point in the establishment of the legal framework for the ownership and commercialization of genetic material was the US Supreme Court 1980 decision *Diamond v. Chakrabarty*, which determined that anything made by man, including living organisms, can be patented. The decision opened the floodgates of biotechnologies, marking a shift in funding from public institutions, which in the past had been the main actors in the research on plants and animals, to private corporations. Biotech focused on profitable endeavors such as genetic modifications, aimed at increasing yields and enhancing the herbicide and pest-resistant properties of commercial crops—especially canola, corn, soybeans, and cotton—that are often cultivated in high-input monocultures and can take advantage of economies of scale. Research dynamics and adoption of GM crops are different in countries like Brazil, Argentina, China, and India, where governments have intervened with policies that prioritize national development.[8] Few efforts have instead targeted crops that are relevant to farmers in developing countries: drought- and pest-resistant high-yield cassava, millet, sorghum, yams, and bananas could positively contribute to food security.

Divergent approaches for risk assessment exist in terms of human health and environmental consequences. The EU embraces a precautionary principle that bars the introduction of GM crops unless tests and trials demonstrate that they do not constitute a threat to humans and the environment. The burden of proof rests on the proponents of the new genetic material. Mistrust toward GMOs is so deeply rooted among European citizens that even after approval at the EU level, whole countries refuse to plant GM crops—or to import products containing GM ingredients, unless they're clearly labeled. Beyond the environmental risks, opponents to GMOs also argue that corporate control over the direction and focus of research has a global impact on biosafety regulations, agricultural policies, development strategies, and global trade. Concerns about these issues led to the 2003 adoption of the Cartagena Protocol on Biosafety to the Convention on Biological Diversity, an international agreement on biosafety that aims to protect biodiversity against the risks of exposure to GMOs. However, trade controversies between countries that opt for preventive procedures and those that embrace and implement production of GM crops can arise, as many governments, including the United States, have opted instead for a more reactionary—rather than precautionary—approach to risk: according to this point of view, new genetic material can be introduced into the environment if it meets acceptable standards of safety, often set by the biotech firms themselves. Interventions take place in case of irrefutable evidence of damage or if problems occur, and the burden of proof shifts to the public.

Regardless of what anyone thinks of the dangers of GM crops, their diffusion may be problematic for farmers who want to stick to non-GM varieties. Pollens do not stop at the edges of fields, and cross-pollination with crops on nearby properties can take place easily. Because GMOs are covered by intellectual property laws, cross-pollination can be considered an infringement. Biotech corporations frame such occurrences in terms of *seed piracy*, in the sense that seeds containing their proprietary and copyrighted genetic material turn up in areas in which they have not been approved and where farmers have not paid the license fees that cover their use. In 1998, Monsanto brought Percy Schmeiser, a Canadian farmer, to court for having illegally saved seeds for the following agricultural cycle. The farmer argued that he was being prosecuted because a Monsanto variety had ended up in his fields accidentally due to cross-pollination, but the courts sided with the biotechnology giant in 2004.[9] Licenses are legal tools meant to discourage farmers from saving seeds from one harvest and using them to grow crops for the following one. Since the early 1990s, technologies have existed for so-called terminator genes—technically known as *genetic use-restriction technology* (GURT)—which would make seed sterile and stop the diffusion of second-generation seeds. However, such technologies are not commercially available, and a moratorium on their use was discussed in 2006 at the United Nations Convention on Biological

Diversity in Curitiba. The very existence of a market for *stealth seeds*, GM seeds that farmers save, exchange, cross-breed, and sell, regardless of biosafety concerns, points to the fact that terminator genes have not been introduced into living plants.[10]

Biotech companies hope that new methods such as *CRISPR-Cas9*, a high-precision genome-editing technique, can change public perceptions about genetic alterations. Bacteria were previously used to insert genes in DNA sequences without much precision (and required long and expensive attempts and trials), but CRISPR-Cas9 doesn't necessarily introduce foreign DNA; instead, it deletes or alters traits already present in the genetic material of the organism. The process is also much cheaper, which over time could make it available to actors other than large biotech corporations. However, opponents to genetic modifications in food point out that a different technology doesn't change the risks for human consumption and for the environment.

Glimpsing the Future of Food Production

Although less intense, similar debates about intellectual property, ownership, accessibility, and governance extend to precision farming, climate-smart agriculture, and e-agriculture. These three descriptors all refer, more or less interchangeably, to the introduction into the rural world of information and communication technologies (ICT), as well as the Internet of Things, the exchange of data among tools, machineries, sensors, software, and mobile applications. The use of cellular platforms in rural areas is one the most promising and viable innovations. Most farmers now have access to simple handheld devices with voice and text capabilities—which is much cheaper than building telephone land lines in remote locations. Building on the diffusion of cell phones among farmers, easy-to-use mobile applications allow them to have a better sense of the current market prices for their crops and the costs of inputs while accessing financing opportunities, insurance tools, and real-time information about weather events. Farmers are introduced to knowledge-intensive practices, including data point analysis and alternative modes of receiving information, seeing, counting, and deciding, which complicate expectations about what *local* and *traditional* mean.

Other technologies are more capital-intensive. Besides geolocating, GPS systems generate images of agricultural lands—which, together with other parcel-identification tools, can be used to determine subsidies for farmers and provide other services (as is already happening in the EU). Drones provide visual information about the state of the fields, the presence of pests and vermin, and the effects of the weather. Software that manages irrigation by regulating valves and pumps contributes to saving water through more efficient distribution. Sensors located in fields send data about soil moisture, temperatures, sun exposure, and crop health to mobile applications that are easily accessed remotely. Sensory technology is also applied in fish and livestock farming to track the behavior and the movements of the animals, monitor their health, and receive updates about pregnancies and births (in the case of livestock). Sensors and tools based on GPS technology have been employed widely in the fishing industry to follow the movements of fish, identify their feeding patterns, and monitor changes in currents and temperatures due to weather events and climate change.

These innovations complicate the fantasy, especially widespread among affluent consumers in postindustrial societies, of traditionally grown crops and traditionally raised animals, generally perceived as safer, healthier, more authentic, and more meaningful. Although innovations can help farmers reduce the use of pesticides and other inputs, the use of cutting-edge technology takes away from the sense of connecting with real people— farmers, shepherds, fishermen, artisans—that intervene in person in food production, getting their hands dirty. Besides challenging consumers' perceptions, the diffusion of high-tech solutions for farming raises serious political issues because they could further concentrate control of the global food system in the hands of a few highly capitalized firms and financial investors. As ICT and IoT generate an unprecedented quantity of data that provides invaluable information for farmers, the industry as a whole, and researchers, concerns arise about how this data is protected and who has access to it. Can the communities involved have a say in how this information is used? Will data be public and free, accessible for a fee, or even sold as an asset? Will its analysis and use be restricted to the tech companies that generate and manage it? As the vulnerability of computer networks becomes painfully clear, could hackers gain access to data about food production, with great risks in terms of food security and food safety? Could information be weaponized to stir financial panic on the commodity markets, to cause dysfunction or paralysis in food-distribution networks, or to make proprietary intellectual property available to anybody?

At the same time, the use of data could bring positive change. Great excitement has accompanied the development of *blockchain* technology—best known for its use in virtual currencies—and its possible applications in supply networks. Using encryption to keep information secure, blockchain constitutes a dispersed database of transactions (known as a *digital ledger*) that all participants in a network have access to. In fact, to be verified and recorded, every transaction must be approved by the networked computers. No single participant has control over the network or can modify transactions independently. Start-ups are applying the new technology to ensure traceability in supply networks through data, confirmations, and certificates, which should make pinpointing critical data easier in the case of a food-safety emergency. Each actor could add information about costs and payments that would keep the whole supply network completely transparent. The risk of fake information would still exist but would be reduced by the integration of geographic information system (GIS) technologies, satellite photography, and peer-to-peer controls. Qualitative data could be included and made available to all users, allowing consumers to verify who the farmers that grew their food are and where they are located.

At a smaller scale, tensions between the productive potential of new technologies and concerns about access, use, and cost also surround the development of *hydroponics*, a method for growing plants without soil that employs solutions of nutrients and water in combination with fluorescent lamps or LED lamps. Allowing for food production in closed and limited spaces, hydroponics has been hailed as a new frontier for urban agriculture and a tool to increase the resilience of urban supply networks in case of disasters (so long as the installations become autonomous in terms of energy thanks to solar panels, wind turbines, or other technologies). Large hydroponics plants have been mounted inside abandoned industrial buildings, as in the case of AeroFarms in Newark, New Jersey. The company has patented a system in which plants grow on cloth, fed by a fine mist and kept growing thanks to LED lighting in a controlled and contained environment; in this way, the company reduces the amount of land, water, and pesticides used while repurposing existing structures.[11] In Singapore, where real estate is a luxury, urban farmers have embraced hydroponics and similar technologies to provide fresh salads and herbs while also integrating composting and fish ponds into aquaponics projects.[12] In such systems, hydroponics are connected to aquaculture, using the waste from fish farming to provide the nutrients necessary for plant growth. There are doubts among consumers about the nutritional content and flavor of plants grown indoors without soil and exposure to natural light, and the impact of hydroponics and aquaponics will greatly depend on the ownership of the technology, its price and accessibility, and its management. Will such productions be controlled by large companies that have the financial means to secure the necessary investments, or could ownership be distributed among citizens?

Consumers and Technology

Innovation also influences aspects of the food system that are much closer to consumers but much less visible. Let's consider just one aspect of the food system: distribution.

Computer networks make it possible for food to get to us smoothly: deliveries are organized, stockrooms are kept full, and we can even shop online. Many of the infrastructures that support the processing, warehousing, delivery, and retail of food are so embedded in supply networks that they may be hard to notice. The invention of refrigerated train cars; the freezing technology that connects industries to domestic freezers through specialized trucks, warehouses, and dedicated structures in retail; and the introduction of forklifts, pallets, and containers into food transportation are just a few of the many innovations that have shaped global distribution in past decades.

Technologies function at different scales, from massive machinery all the way to the most intimate dimensions of our bodies. Wearable appliances as small as watches now can easily monitor our movements, our blood pressure, and the intensity of our exercise. We can store and carry easy-to-administer medications in case we eat something that provokes an allergic reaction or, worse, an anaphylactic shock. We can ingest cameras to check how our stomachs and intestines digest the food we eat.[13] Nanotechnologies constitute a constantly expanding frontier, creating opportunities to track our physiology on an unprecedented detailed scale. Research is closely looking at our intestinal *microbiota*—that is, the "ecological community of commensal, symbiotic, and pathogenic microorganisms" that share our body space and which is now indicated as both the possible cause of and the solution to many health problems.[14] At a macro level, innovation takes inspiration from nature to create processes that mimic activities and metabolic processes of nature in its ecological complexity, from microorganisms in the soil to the use of cover crops that disrupt the growth of pathogens after the harvest. Fungi and algae are being studied as tools to produce biofuels, compost waste, and even provide biodegradable building materials. Meat protein is being grown in labs and tests conducted to produce it commercially, while plant-based burgers designed to look, smell, and taste much like beef already are sold in restaurants.[15]

Kitchen appliances are food-related technologies that constantly interact with humans without much tension, especially when they offer convenience and efficiency. Most consumers seem to have gotten over any diffidence toward the introduction of frozen food in the 1950s and microwaves in the 1980s, which required profound cultural changes with regard to ideas about food quality, freshness, and safety, as well as the agency of the cook. Today, innovations such as sous vide machines, convection ovens, induction burners, and digital refrigeration monitoring can be found both in domestic and professional kitchens. When applied to food manufacturing, restaurants, and large institutions, such innovations can offer more efficient use of ingredients, inputs, and energy. Other, apparently more fanciful appliances are met with reactions that range from curiosity to amusement. Fridges can keep tabs on what food is going bad inside or what products are running out, connecting with online grocery shops that arrange deliveries of what's needed. Such an application of IoT may come across as far from essential, but it works well for individuals who forget about food, like patients suffering from Alzheimer's disease or dementia, and helps them to eat properly, improving their health and relieving family and friends from some worries. Domestic appliances can provide solutions that improve quality of life for people with disabilities. Kitchenware and silverware are being designed to allow blind individuals to eat more easily, and 3-D printers might let friends and family share recipes and actual food at a distance by using the same files to print edible matter.

Food design, a new field of research and practice within the discipline of design, is developing as an answer to these opportunities and challenges through interaction with chefs, producers, and food-studies scholars. The field is growing fast in Western Europe and South America and less quickly in North America, Asia (with the exception of East Asia), and Africa. As defined by Food Design North America (of which I am among the founders), *food design* "includes any action that can improve our relationship with food individually or collectively. These actions can relate to the design of food products, materials, practices, environments, systems, processes and experiences."[16] The association clarifies that the working definition needs to be considered as a point of departure, not a conclusion, because the goal is to open up dialogues rather than offering schematic or reductionist demarcations. In recent years, design has turned its attention to all aspects of the food we produce and eat, from tableware to restaurant design, from experience to networks. This interest is part of the evolution of design itself, which has expanded its horizons from objects and spaces to include knowledge-intensive forms of processes, services, and systems. Designers that opt for human-centered innovation participate in the development of projects that recognize the priorities, values, and needs of all the actors involved, especially those whose voices are least heard. These projects tend to consider complex contexts and situations to test prototypes that can then be improved through feedback from users and local communities. This reflects a change in the involvement of stakeholders, who move from being mere recipients of the professional interventions of designers to becoming codesigners and participants.

Such approaches could guide new technologies to harmonize the need for greater food availability with efforts to ensure long-term sustainability and to reflect the preferences of consumers. Will new technologies usher in a greater democratization in the food system, or will they intensify the inequalities between the haves and the have-nots? Is technology the only way to improve efficiency and yields in food production? More importantly, is producing more the single most urgent priority? These questions are crucial at a time when, despite the growing availability, accessibility, and affordability of food, many individuals, families, and whole communities struggle to get proper nourishment, as we will discuss in the next chapter.

HUNGER AND FOOD SECURITY

A woman is in line at a food bank to get groceries to feed her family; the volunteer at the counter, warm and spontaneous, tries to make her feel welcomed. A farmer in a drought-stricken area holds in her hand the few cobs of corn she managed to grow: she is proud, but she also knows that trouble is coming. A man is protesting on the street because of the sudden increase in the price of bread; the police in riot gear stand between him and a bakery. A young boy with a little cash in his hand is trying to decide what to buy in a small urban grocery store, which only sells high-calorie, prepackaged food. A little girl is dreading to have lunch in her school cafeteria, knowing that her classmates will taunt her for taking advantage of the free food provided by the government. A child with a distended stomach is crying in desperation, while a nurse attends her. People in a war-ravaged landscape are waiting for the arrival of emergency food.

These images are so pervasive in popular culture that we may become anesthetized to other humans' suffering, wherever it may take place. We can easily picture these situations: media have made sure that we are familiar with these kinds of vignettes, to the point that we may consider them inevitable realities that will never disappear. As disturbing as these images may be, the lived experience of hunger is hard to fathom. What does insufficient nutrition do to a person, emotionally and physically? What are the long-term cultural and social consequences of the prolonged lack of access to sufficient nourishment?

Food deprivation happens in different ways, at different levels of gravity, and due to different problems. This complexity makes the issue hard to define and thus to tackle effectively. According to the FAO, "Food security exists when all people, at all times, have physical and economic access to sufficient, safe, and nutritious food to meet their dietary needs and food preferences for an active and healthy life. The four pillars of food security are availability, stability of supply, access and utilization."[1] In other words, food should be constantly available in sufficient quantity and quality for everybody; physically and economically accessible; healthy; culturally acceptable in the context in which it is consumed; and made available to those who can actually transform it into adequate nutrition for themselves and others.

In this chapter, we'll explore how *food insecurity* (i.e., the lack of food security at any level and scale) is activated, interpreted, or ignored as a political issue, both in its less dangerous expressions and when it turns into hunger and famine. Although we will focus on policy and politics, we can't forget that food insecurity is not only an economic and social issue, but also deeply affects the individuals and the communities that experience it. Physical sufferance, emotional vulnerability, a sense of shame, social isolation, anger, and desperation are among the less visible and more devastating consequences. Depending on whether such a condition is interpreted as an individual issue or as the outcome of broad systemic problems that go well beyond food, proposed solutions can vary from charity and ad hoc interventions that address emergencies to structural and long-term policies at the local, national, and international levels.

Food as a Human Right

Famine and starvation are dreadful and life-threatening, taking their toll on physiology and the mental health of individuals and impacting the well-being of families and nations.[2] Unfortunately, such occurrences are not rare, caused by circumstances as diverse as wars, natural disasters, social injustice, and racism. In the 1840s, a blight destroyed the potato harvest of Irish farmers for several years, forcing many to leave the island to survive.[3] In the 1870s, the British colonies in India endured a devastating famine due in part to climate circumstances, but also to the exploitative policies of the British Raj.[4] Starvation was rampant in the Ukraine during the Stalin years, connected to misguided agricultural policies and political decisions. In Jewish ghettos, Nazi concentration camps, and Japanese prisoner of war camps during World War II, many victims died from lack of food because they were considered second-class human beings.[5] More recent instances include the famine that hit China between 1958 and 1961, caused by Mao Zedong's disastrous industrialization policies and their consequences in the countryside; widespread starvation caused by the attempted secession of Biafra from Nigeria in the late 1960s; and, in the twenty-first century, the famines in the Sahel, Yemen, and South Sudan, all caused by conflicts.

Hunger is a scourge that affects both developed and developing countries, although it obviously manifests itself differently and the responses vary depending on the context. Food plays an important role in achieving the objectives the United Nations identified in 2015 with the adoption of the seventeen Sustainable Development Goals of the 2030 Agenda for Sustainable Development.[6] Zero Hunger constitutes a goal in itself, whereas other goals emphasize ensuring sufficient access to water

Food plays an important role in achieving the objectives the United Nations identified in 2015 with the adoption of the seventeen Sustainable Development Goals of the 2030 Agenda for Sustainable Development. Zero Hunger constitutes a goal in itself.

for everybody, integrating rural and urban food systems, and limiting soil degradation and the loss of biodiversity, among other measures. This call to action is directed to all countries, regardless of their GDP and their standard of life.

Besides eliminating hunger as the most destructive manifestation of food insecurity, a recurring element across several Sustainable Development Goals is the need for appropriate nutrition to ensure cultural, social, and economic development. Making sure that infants and young children are well fed is a priority, as is ensuring adequate nutrition for pregnant women. Lack of adequate prenatal nutrition leads to stunting and impairments, both mental and physical. Although the number of stunted and wasted children has diminished in recent years, the rate of obesity is on the rise, generating different but not less harmful forms of malnutrition. The growth of obesity among the food insecure is only apparently a paradox. Changes in dietary patterns with increased consumption of calorie-rich, nutrient-poor, and highly processed foods are among the factors contributing to this phenomenon. FAO also cites as issues "women's educational level; resources allocated to national policies and programs for maternal, infant and young child nutrition; access to clean water, basic sanitation and quality health services; lifestyle; food environment; and culture."[7]

Food has been a central concern for the United Nations since its inception. After the disasters of World War II, the international community hoped that cooperation could improve the living conditions of humanity as a whole. In fact, three agencies—all based in Rome, Italy—were founded to take care of different aspects: FAO, the overall goal of which is to defeat hunger; the World Food Programme (WFP), which intervenes in cases of specific emergencies; and the International Fund for Agricultural Development (IFAD), which supports projects to achieve inclusive and sustainable rural transformations. In the United Nations framework, food is a human right, as stated in Article 25 of the 1948 Universal Declaration of Human Rights, Article 11 of the 1966 International Covenant on Economic Social and Cultural Rights, and Articles 24 and 27 of the 1989 Convention on the Rights of the Child. These international instruments impose obligations on the states that signed them to ensure the progressive realization of every individual's right to adequate food by providing access and safety, as well as nutritional quality, availability, and affordability.[8]

Food should never be used as a tool for political and economic pressure, regardless of sex, age, race, color, religion, political or other opinion, national or social origin, language, or any other status. Effective policies focusing on food security are the necessary precondition for the fruition of the right to food, which is connected to other human rights, such as the right to life, the right to health, the right to water, the right to adequate housing, and the right to work. Yet food security remains an elusive goal at the global level, even in communities that appear well-fed.

Food Security: A Political Issue

After a steady decline in the first years of the twenty-first century, according to the FAO, food insecurity is again on the rise: the number of malnourished individuals around the world increased from 777 million in 2015 to 815 million in 2017. We can only consider these figures a rough approximation as they're based on aggregated data about average calorie availability that doesn't provide information on individuals and families, their actual needs, and how they cope with them. Data on stunted children are relatively more reliable because estimates derive from the measurement of actual individuals. Despite these difficulties, crafting reliable metrics and gathering data about hunger is central to the political negotiations that may prevent or support the launch of effective policies and interventions. Private organizations also contribute to design instruments for the assessment of food security, such as the Global Food Security Index launched by the Economist Intelligence Unit with the support of DuPont (a company that is likely to see a strong and expanding agriculture as an opportunity to sell more products, from seeds to pesticides).[9]

Data analysis points to conflicts as the main reason for the spike in food insecurity since 2010, especially in sub-Saharan Africa and Western Asia. Although violence causes the displacement of large populations, generating migration flows that destabilize whole regions, its effects are more devastating in areas where inadequate institutional arrangements do not support consumers and producers through a viable and stable local food system. It can be argued that long-term consequences of failed policies share great responsibilities in creating emergency situations. Political instability is often compounded by increasing unpredictability in weather patterns; droughts and floods have a greater impact on agricultural production, at times forcing farmers to abandon their land. Moreover, countries that depend on raw material exports as their leading source of income have seen prices of commodities—from oil to metals—decrease, reducing the government capacity to intervene against food price instability through aid and subsidies.

Of course, hunger is not a new issue facing humankind. A physiological consequence of inadequate nutrition, it's also determined by cultural categories and political power struggles. Historian Martin Bruegel observes: "Different social environments elaborate and live according to their own notions of what is adequate nourishment. ... Each social class carries its own definition of what is necessary, of what is decent in order to belong to the group, to find one's place within it, and to avoid losing face. ... Hunger, in the sense of lack, can be experienced when there are enough calories and food. This perceived privation, and not the metabolic reality, guides human behavior."[10] Starving people at times accept their condition with resignation, although their plight can easily turn into widespread social unrest under politically unstable circumstances.

The fear of dying for lack of food has constantly generated anxiety during most of human history. It manifested itself, for instance, in compensatory feasts—which also constituted expressions of culture and social connectivity—and in the popular fantasy of Cockaigne, the legendary land that medieval inhabitants of Europe imagined as constantly full of free and abundant food. The elites exorcised similar concerns through conspicuous consumption, by displaying abundance and even extravagance in banquets and public occasions: fresh vegetables and fish, inherently impermanent and easy to spoil, as well as ice or snow to cool beverages were proudly offered to guests. Power defined itself as freedom from lack of food and freedom of excess and wastefulness. Only with the affirmation of bourgeois taste in the nineteenth century did refinement and, to a certain extent, restraint become synonymous with affluence: quality and exclusiveness were more relevant than sheer quantity to express social and cultural distinction.

Civilizations employed different cultural and social strategies to ensure sufficient food supplies and confirm the legitimacy of power structures. Social instability due to food shortages, which could easily turn into riots or, at times, revolutions, was a formidable incentive for governments to provide adequate provisions to its citizens, especially in urban centers where political opposition could more easily emerge and become organized. The Roman Empire constantly secured wheat-producing lands to feed the restless populace of the capital, which received free or subsidized grains. The Ottoman Empire developed soup kitchens, while the Qing dynasty established a complex system of public granaries in China to move food rapidly around the country when necessary. Precolonial sub-Saharan African empires supported cross-cultural long-distance trade to overcome environmental limitations and a consequent lack of nutritional diversity. These concrete efforts were often supported by ideological propaganda meant to depict the state as a generous benefactor. In fact, if framed in socially acceptable terms, food scarcity and high prices of staples do not necessarily lead to turmoil. Conversely, periods when food is available can be marked by social instability fostered by perceived scarcity or, more often, a sense of unjust distribution. Cultural perceptions are crucial in determining social reactions and political

The Roman Empire constantly secured wheat-producing lands to feed the restless populace of the capital, which received free or subsidized grains. The Ottoman Empire developed soup kitchens, while the Qing dynasty established a complex system of public granaries in China to move food rapidly around the country when necessary.

mobilization, not only in cases of severe famine but also when responding to various degrees of food insecurity.

Cultural Perceptions

Food insecurity is an overwhelming and multilayered issue, endemic around the globe regardless of countries' wealth or power. It's easy for individual citizens or civil society groups to feel powerless and consider it a problem that will always be there, whatever they may try to do. Media may focus on a minority of individuals—regardless of their geographical location—whose poverty is apparent while ignoring those who struggle in secret, a growing segment of the population in the Global North. When close to home, food insecurity may end up remaining almost invisible. Poverty and hunger are not proper topics to discuss in polite company.

Nobody should die of hunger. Especially when it comes to children, wherever they may be, allowing them to suffer is considered an unforgivable sin that stains our civilization. There is worldwide cultural and political agreement on these basic tenets, even among those who fully embrace the narrative—especially strong in the United States— that glorifies self-made individuals who pull themselves up by their own bootstraps. Recognizable in US culture since its inception—it is enough to read Benjamin Franklin's autobiography or Horatio Alger's rags-to-riches novels—the idea that individuals are responsible for their present conditions and their future perspectives is central in the capitalist approach to the economy and the market. Its influence has expanded worldwide thanks to the influence of the United States and other industrialized countries. In this perspective, personal choices make people more or less deserving of success or failure. From the late 1970s, political propaganda in the United States derogatorily labeled women who relied on the public support system *welfare queens*, accusing them of taking advantage of taxpayers' generosity. The myth that assistance recipients are lazy is used as an excuse to deprive the weakest in society of their means for survival.

In this landscape, well-meaning individuals may feel that the only way they can contribute to food security is by participating in interventions like food drives or donations—especially around the holidays, when the injustice of abject poverty becomes harder to ignore. Volunteers and activists who participate in all sorts of anti-hunger initiatives show amazing generosity and passion. However, although organized with the best intentions, these efforts emphasize temporary solutions while distracting from the real issues underlying hunger and malnutrition, which require more complex and far-reaching policies.[11]

Although antihunger initiatives such as food banks and soup kitchens play a crucial role in mitigating the worst aspects of food insecurity, by focusing exclusively on emergency measures we risk depoliticizing the issue, with the consequence that institutions and governments may not feel pressure from public opinion to deal with the underlying problems causing individuals and families to experience food insecurity in the first place.[12] Moreover, the organizations supporting food banks and soup kitchens often are partly funded by large corporations, including those in the food industry, which provide money and food donations in exchange for political goodwill and favorable public relations. The contradiction is evident when we examine the impact of corporate philanthropy on concealing the responsibilities that corporations themselves may have for causing the problems they try to assuage.[13]

Principles and actions to eradicate hunger—both nationally and internationally—vary enormously. Should governments support private efforts to avoid the worst for those who can't afford to buy food? Or should they instead intervene in the functioning of food production and distribution, the job market, wages, housing, healthcare, and access to education, among other factors that impact—directly and indirectly—the weakest segments of the populations? Is the main goal charity or social justice? Should we address symptoms or deal with deep causes through far-reaching reforms? To deal with the problem of food insecurity at its root, it's necessary to examine the food system in its complexity in ways that go well beyond the contributions, as generous as they may be, that any individual or community can provide.

Reframing Hunger

Food insecurity is at the core of important and heated political debates. The same tensions reverberate in economic and social research focusing on lack of food, its causes, and its consequences. You may hear people worry that there is not enough food produced, that there are too many humans on the planet, and that in a short time we won't have enough to eat. The mainstream answer to this concern is to produce more food, with technology and scientific innovation constituting the go-to solution.

What if hunger is instead an effect of misdistribution, rather than lack of food? What if we produce enough food, but people don't have the means or the opportunities to acquire it? If that is the case, strategies should focus on what people need in terms of income, access, and support to grow or buy food, including private and public safety networks. This approach is common among those who take into consideration cultural, social, and political aspects of the food system, looking beyond its productive features. Among these, economist and Noble Prize laureate Amartya Sen introduced a paradigm that frames hunger-related issues in terms of *entitlements*: the wages, exchanges, productive activities, and support that individuals, families, and communities need to secure access to food. For Sen, "a person's ability to command food—indeed, to command any commodity he wishes to acquire or retain—depends on the entitlement relations that govern possessions and use in that society. It depends on what he owns, what exchange possibilities are offered to him, what is given to him for free, and what is taken away from him. ... Food supply is only one influence among many affecting his entitlement relations."[14] Building on Sen's perspective, Olivier De Schutter, formerly the United Nations special rapporteur on the right to food, explains that "individuals can secure access to food (a) by earning incomes from employment or self-employment; (b) through social transfers; or (c) by producing their own food, for those who have access to land and other productive resources."[15]

If a person works as a miner and the mine is shut down suddenly because it is exhausted or its owner has a new business plan, his opportunities for getting enough income to buy food—or anything else, for that matter—plummet. Because eating is just one need among others, such as a home, utilities, clothes, and healthcare, survival turns into a balancing act. Farmers may find themselves in dire straits not because they do not have a good harvest, but because the market price for their crops is too low to ensure a decent livelihood. Securing entitlements means looking at wider cultural, social, economic, and political dynamics beyond food.

The Most Vulnerable

This approach is far from being univocally embraced. Cultural and political biases determine perceptions about who deserves support and who does not. Besides the obvious class judgment, racial and ethnic undertones are right below the surface, if not out in the open. Migrants and refugees often suffer the brunt of this rhetoric while they struggle to adapt to host countries that do not necessary welcome them. Affluent countries are not always ready—and often not willing—to take care of economic and political refugees. Their presence is felt as a burden, and making sure they have access to food that is culturally acceptable to them is perceived as a liberal weakness that entitles immigrants to have expectations they shouldn't have in their situation.

In some countries, indigenous communities, which may have their own cultural categories about what constitutes adequate food, often suffer from food insecurity as the result of centuries of exclusion, colonization, and expropriation of lands and other natural resources. Ethnic minorities in Vietnam have been displaced in large numbers from their traditional areas in the highlands to make room for coffee plantations, in which they can only work as labor, if anything at all. Cultural bias and prejudice in terms of race and ethnicity impact who has access to finance, land tenure, and food-related businesses. In the United States, since the end of the Civil War, African American farmers have found accessing credit and government support more difficult than their white peers.[16] In these cases, assertive policies are required to allow disadvantaged groups to have access to and control over their resources.

In other contexts, smallholders are a particularly vulnerable category that is overlooked when national authorities focus their attention on the growing urban population of big megalopolises, especially in the Global South. Support in the face of weather-related disasters, recessions, and the consequences of international trade liberalization should be provided so that rural dwellers can stay in their places of origin instead of moving to cities in search of jobs. Moreover, research and development initiatives should be launched that respond to the specific needs of small farmers in terms of technology, logistics, management, education, and infrastructure.

Harmful biases are connected to gender as well. In many rural environments, women are in charge of crop cultivations and food production, not only for subsistence but also for the market, both selling locally and participating in the production of cash crops for export. However, due to preconceptions about gender, their role is often hidden, if not denied, and men become the beneficiaries of development projects and investment. Male family members are considered economic actors, enjoying social standing and financial support even when they are not involved in the business or squander resources. In situations of poverty, these issues can become a source of tension and at times violence within households. Shifting perceptions about social roles is not enough to improve women's livelihoods. The power relations that keep women in inferior positions need to change to redistribute property rights, modify decision-making processes within the household, and eliminate the structural conditions that restrict women's access to training, financial support, and loans. When they have control over the household budget, women tend to prioritize spending on food rather than other expenses, often putting their spouses' and children's nutritional needs before their own. These situations are particularly taxing on women when they are the breadwinners and in charge of food procurement and preparation.

Age discrimination is another important factor to take into consideration. Not only the very young but also the elderly are at particular risk. Especially where senior citizens do not enjoy high status and respect as wise and valuable members of society, they are often forgotten by both their own families and public institutions. If they don't have access to retirement plans and affordable health care, they end up experiencing constant food insecurity. To avoid these situations, in some countries the retirees and the elderly have formed associations that can exert noticeable lobbying power thanks to their sheer numbers. AARP, a US association for retirees, constantly maintains pressure on politicians on behalf of their members and the over-fifty population in general; it also runs a foundation that takes care of members in need, also in terms of food security. Meals on Wheels, which delivers meals to those who can't cook or leave their homes, provides food to numerous elderly people in the United Kingdom, Canada, Australia, the United States, and Ireland.

Support Programs in Industrialized Countries

Although populations lacking access to proper nutrition exist in all countries, situations of food insecurity in industrialized countries tend to be relatively less intense, compared to life-threatening famines. Even governments that do not particularly prioritize citizen welfare provide special support to pregnant women and mothers, infants, and small children. School meals are among the most common schemes. However, affluent societies are not necessarily more equitable, even when, as in the United States, they have the means to create safety networks.[17] Each country adopts policies that reflect specific contexts, social dynamics, and political tensions. Where government subsidies and support programs exist, they are always subject to political negotiations, as are the methodologies used to measure food insecurity. The quantity of the funds allotted for these interventions, the categories of population to which they apply, and the mechanisms through which they are distributed vary enormously, often exposed to the vagaries of politics and economic cycles.

Furthermore, food and funds are distributed only to those whose income places them under administratively established poverty lines, which are at times so low that even a small income from a part-time job may preclude potential recipients from getting what they need. The requirements may be stringent also in terms of demonstrating attempts at finding employment or reviewing a person's housing situation, number of household members, and so on. In the United States, many workers in the food industry—for example, farm labor, factory personnel slaughtering animals or processing food, and fast-food employees—have such meager incomes that they qualify for food support, creating a paradox in which taxpayers practically subsidize private companies to exploit their workers and keep wages low. The administrative process to qualify for support can be complex and time-consuming, creating a substantial hindrance for individuals who may already have little time left from multiple jobs and may be too overwhelmed by their situation to properly take care of the necessary paperwork. On the other hand, such processes are set up as filters to make sure that only those who really need help get it. As we already discussed, cultural biases about poverty have a noticeable impact on programs that politicians have to convince their constituencies to maintain.

At times, support isn't allocated directly to recipients but instead targets their food environments. For instance, *food deserts*—areas where fresh and nutritious food isn't available, dominated instead by a prevalence of outlets selling fast food or highly processed, prepackaged products—have become an urgent problem in the cities of the Global North (but also in the quickly expanding shantytowns that surround large cities, from Johannesburg to Delhi, from Rio de Janeiro to Bogota). Such situations can become the target of interventions by city governments, including zoning regulations that require the presence of fresh food sale points in residential real estate. Tax breaks may be provided to companies for opening stores and supermarkets in underserved neighborhoods. In some cities in the United States, recipients of the Supplemental Nutrition Assistance Program (SNAP; the federal scheme for the reduction of food insecurity) can use some of their SNAP funds to buy fresh vegetables and fruits at subsidized prices from local farmers' markets. Local authorities also create small markets or street vendor networks that deliver fresh food to locations where there are few stores carrying those kinds of items.

However, recent research has questioned the tenets behind the very concept of food deserts and their value as a policy goal in industrialized countries, showing instead a strong correlation among income, educational levels, and preferences for healthy and unhealthy foods,[18] meaning that hunger may exist also where food is available. Moreover, the food desert label discounts other food production and exchange networks that may not be immediately visible. Efforts to make fresh food available take place at all levels: Community gardens and urban farms strive to produce fresh vegetables and fruit, often taking advantage of abandoned spaces, while providing social activities in the area. Families, friends, and neighbors often organize collective transportation to the nearest outlets of fresh food or share produce that relatives may send from the nearby countryside.

Food insecurity also can be generated by dynamics that may appear overall positive. In many cities, *gentrification*, the process through which whole neighborhoods are revitalized through the influx of higher-income inhabitants, has undesirable collateral effects. The arrival of new dwellers in previously low-income neighborhoods often pushes real estate, rent, services, and food costs up.

Small farm-to-table restaurants, gourmet cafes, and natural food stores open to cater to the needs and preferences of the newcomers. The markets that cities had built in previous decades to provide food for local dwellers of all walks of life are turned into glamorous food halls, leisure places for affluent consumers and tourists. Abandoned factories and whole neighborhoods previously dedicated to industrial activities become hubs for food innovation, creative manufacturing, and intriguing new restaurants. However, prices inevitably increase, making finding affordable food difficult. The changes often end up forcing the poorest segments of the preexisting communities to move to more affordable destinations.

Fighting Hunger in the Global South

Ensuring the food security of large populations poses even greater challenges to Global South countries, due to inadequate institutional arrangements, lack of cash, and few opportunities to borrow money on the international financial market. Nevertheless, all governments focus on their poorest populations' most urgent needs, such as food, water, and medical aid. India's constitution, for instance, includes the right to food, and in 2013 the national government introduced the National Food Security Act, which guarantees subsidized prices for staples such as rice, wheat, and millet for eligible families, identified state by state. The act also provides free cereals for many categories of children, pregnant women, and breastfeeding mothers. In 2003, Brazil launched *Fome Zero* (Zero Hunger), a set of programs meant to address aspects of entitlements failures in various sectors. Among other measures, it comprises price stabilization; direct financial help for needy families; support for small-scale farming, including purchases by schools and other public institutions; creation of water reservoirs in the most arid areas of the country; and nutritional education. Unfortunately, due to Brazil's recent political and economic crisis, the funding for many of the programs is being reduced, and some initiatives are being dismantled.

Most countries also invest in medium- and long-term development. Efforts may include better management of trade and imports, as well as strategic reserves of grains and other staples. Various policies emphasize education, technical training, risk management, farming cooperative formation, and infrastructures. Soil and water conservation are also targeted, together with research and development aimed at improving local, drought-resisting, high-yield crop varieties (not necessarily through genetic modification). Contingency plans are put into place to deal with sudden climate- or conflict-related crises. Such structural interventions are frequently supported by international aid, which contributes to addressing chronic food insecurity. This kind of aid, which was central in the decades after World War II, has declined from the 1970s, as we'll discuss in chapter 7; aid now focuses instead on acute crises.

International aid plays a crucial role in addressing emergencies during political crises and natural disasters. However, although public and private organizations help mitigate the worst consequences of food insecurity, certain interventions need to be rethought. The uninterrupted flow of international aid leads to forms of dependency, when not properly managed, or can be funneled into self-enrichment schemes for corrupted officials. Instead of buying surplus crops from their farmers to be shipped to areas where food is needed, Global North governments could directly invest money to support the development of agriculture in those same areas, allowing local farmers to make a living. In fact, food from international agencies at times undercuts local food producers because it floods the market at lower prices. While cheaper food favors consumers and urban dwellers, it tends to have negative consequences among food producers, who cannot compete. Crisis mitigation can't be the only goal. The International Red Cross and Red Crescent Movement, for instance, has founded a climate center, with the goal of focusing on better early-warning, risk-reduction, and climate-smart programs for agriculture, which can help farmers understand the complex connections between climate change and food production and better deal with emergencies.[19]

However, in recent years, worldwide food crises have been the result of broad global dynamics that are not directly connected to botched national policies, natural disasters, political violence, or decreases in food production. The sudden spikes in commodity prices during the 2007 to 2008 food crisis, which caused riots in locations as diverse as Egypt, Indonesia, and Yemen, have been attributed to factors such as the growing interest in biofuels, the financialization of food commodities, the shifts in food consumption patterns (especially in large countries such as China and India), and the panic about possible scarcity that made some countries stop exporting crops. These events point to the centrality of transnational flows of goods, money, people, and technology in determining not only food security but also the future of the global food system.

WHAT HAPPENS NEXT?

Globalization has been one of the major phenomena shaping our present-day food system, together with environmental changes, political tensions and transformations, and cultural shifts that include the mediatization of food and its increasing relevance in public discourse. Well-established but always evolving global dynamics determine the way we grow, trade, sell, and eat food. Affluent shoppers in London, New York, or Shanghai, wooed by promises of well-being, can consume a superfood crop because specific technologies allow it to travel to its end destination from its place of origin. In those locations, rural communities have seen their labor arrangements, social customs, and dietary patterns change to redirect their production toward export, with immediate economic, political, and public health consequences. In previous chapters, we discussed aspects as diverse as nutrition, the environment, technology, and hunger, which all share a common trait: they are influenced by structures and processes that operate across national borders. To what extent are these elements ingrained in the system? How do they evolve? In this chapter, we'll discuss how today's realities may impact our future. What can we do, as consumers and as citizens, to influence such developments and to introduce the transformations that our food system needs?

Human Mobility

Burgers, pizza, falafel, sushi, burritos, kebabs: these are just few of the meals that have become common and affordable fare in industrialized countries and beyond. These foods used to be limited to large cities outside their native cultures, but they're now available in small towns as well, and, at times, in the countryside. They represent encountering different culinary traditions through hybridization, adaptation, and, often, appropriation. Moreover, these dishes have become symbols of cosmopolitanism and affluence in the metropolises of the Global South, from Mumbai to Buenos Aires, expressing openness to other cultures, a sense of curiosity, and a desire for greater choices and new flavors. As consumption of "ethnic" food spreads among consumers, knowledge about foreign culinary traditions has turned into currency in terms of *cultural capital*—that is, those intangible assets connected with a person's experience or education that can be used to improve her or his social standing. Knowledge-based expertise has become so important in contemporary food discourse that food scholars Keith Lebesco and Peter Naccarato have defined it as *culinary capital*.[1]

The global circulation of plants, animals, and dishes comes with a circulation of people, leading to social and cultural repercussions that play a central role in shaping the future of the global food system. Immigrants don't limit themselves to opening restaurants or food stores. Once they arrive in a new country, following their desire for a better life, they may find employment in the expansion of crop cultivations or in specific sectors of food manufacturing, living in areas where their presence can generate tension. These newcomers—especially if they're undocumented—are willing to work in insecure conditions and for low wages. Workers who do not accept excessively low pay and producers who can't compete are pushed out of the market. Exploited, isolated, and unable to access better jobs, immigrant workers often are resented, treated as foreign elements in the social body, and they can become the object of virulent forms of racism and xenophobia. Haitian sugarcane workers in the Dominican Republic, fruit and vegetable pickers from sub-Saharan Africa in southern Europe, Nicaraguan banana workers in processing and packaging plants in Costa Rica, and

Hispanic labor in slaughterhouses in the United States all are blatant examples of these dynamics. Various countries issue temporary visas for seasonal workers, but these visas often can't meet the needs of the food-production sector.

Food can constitute both an opportunity and an obstacle for immigrants to climb the social ladder. In the nineteenth century, US mainstream society was suspicious of foreign culinary customs. As early as the 1850s, the Chinese settling on the West Coast during the gold rush and the expansion of the railway network were criticized for their excessive consumption of rice and vegetables instead of "manly" meat and more "civilized" staples. However, over time they managed to open small restaurants for the locals, turning an invented dish, chop suey, into a well-known specialty. A few decades later, it was Italian food's turn to be considered smelly, not nourishing, and too vegetable and grain heavy; well-meaning social workers tried—with little success—to impose more "American" eating patterns on the Italians. Yet over time pizza and pasta have become global staples, and now Italian cuisine enjoys prestige and commercial success. Similar reactions took place with almost every new wave of immigrants that tried to assimilate into the United States.[2] Time and again, immigrant *foodways* were integrated into local repertories, though at different levels of glamor and prestige. Not many Americans would be willing to spend much on a Chinese or Mexican meal, which are generally perceived as cheap and unpretentious. Japanese and Italian cuisine have reached a much higher status, with establishments ranging from modest eateries to fine-dining restaurants.[3] Relative newcomers to the world culinary stage, like Peruvian, Korean, and Thai cuisines, are receiving growing attention.

Species on the Move

The movement of crops and animal species also plays a crucial role in constantly changing the food system. Bioprospectors from large pharmaceutical corporations and food industries constantly scout locations around the world to identify plants that can be exploited commercially. These episodes are so pervasive that the 1992 Convention on Biological Diversity included articles to limit and regulate them. Expanding this approach, the 2010 Nagoya Protocol has established procedures for access to and benefit sharing of genetic material the conservation and use of which can be attributed to traditional or tribal populations. Experiments to safeguard traditional knowledge through collaborations among communities, research institutions, and industries have succeeded in India, as in the case of the *arogyapacha* medicinal plant, grown by the Kani tribe in Kerala, the fruits of which fight fatigue. However, these occurrences are still rare, as Western companies frequently

Bioprospectors from large pharmaceutical corporations and food industries constantly scout locations around the world to identify plants that can be exploited commercially.

succeed in patenting plant varieties originally domesticated and selected by indigenous cultures.[4]

Crop transfers have taken place since the beginning of agriculture. Wheat and barley, domesticated in the Middle East, found their way to China before the first millennium BCE. Eggplants and spinach, probably domesticated in India, spread to the Mediterranean during the expansion of the Muslim empire from the seventh century CE. Such diffusion was extremely slow and only loosely coordinated by political powers due to limited technology and means of transportation. Everything changed following the fifteenth century's European explorations of the coasts of Africa and the Indian Ocean, and later the Americas and Oceania. The establishment of European trading posts and settlement colonies caused unplanned transfers of plants, animals, and microorganisms between the New World and the Old World in the phenomenon known as the *Columbian exchange*.

Imperial powers—the example of which transnational corporations have more recently followed—soon found that moving crops to where they could better control production and distribution according to their economic and political needs was convenient and efficient. These policies have been described as *ecological imperialism*.[5] Although the introduction of a new crop variety in a location can trigger a boom in food production, it can have unknown consequences in terms of environmental and social sustainability. The introduction of corn into the Old World in the sixteenth century allowed for the expansion of agriculture to marginal lands, increased food availability, and stimulated demographic growth. The diffusion of sweet potatoes in China from the sixteenth century is one of the factors behind the population explosion in the following centuries that eventually led to the end of the Chinese empire. Kiwi was a curiosity in Italy until the 1970s; now the country has become one of the largest producers in the world. Coffee recently has been planted in the highlands of Vietnam, causing the displacement of ethnic minorities and massive deforestation while stimulating a massive export boom. These transfers of crops are likely to continue in the future, in part as a response to the changing environmental conditions caused by climate change.

Complex ecologies and global interconnections make supply networks porous and vulnerable. All sorts of microorganisms travel with plants and animals. The transmission of plant blights can unleash havoc in agricultural production across continents, as in the case of the Panama disease, which in the 1950s devastated the Gros Michel banana variety, the most common at the time. The disaster forced growers to adopt the Cavendish variety, which now is being threatened in turn by new strains of the same Panama disease. In fact, the infection is already affecting cultivation in South and Southeast

Asia, stimulating feverish research into new, more resistant varieties. Similarly, coffee production is besieged by various species-specific diseases, which—although little-known among the public—are causing anxiety in the supply network. Producers and distributors are scrambling to stop their propagation across borders and to find new varieties that may offer possible alternatives. Similarly, the quick dispersal across continents of pathogens affecting animals, such as the avian flu or mad cow disease, has created profound changes not only in consumers' preferences but also in methods of production and prevention.

Fueled by news about occurrences of contagion and food scares around the world, concerns about food-borne viruses and pests coming from faraway places are mounting. Although consumers generally appreciate wider choices in terms of ingredients, products, dishes, and culinary styles, a certain ambivalence still lingers in the face of elements that may be only marginally familiar or that have only recently entered their sphere of experience. As often happens when it comes to food, which penetrates the intimacy of our bodies through ingestion, a certain fear of the unknown may counterbalance curiosity and excitement for novelties.[6] Because of the dazzling variety of available foods, as well as the uncertain outcomes of globalization, individuals and communities at times express anxieties about the possible dilution and the eventual erasure of their specificities and unique cultural identities. Self-sufficiency, often expressed through the desire for traditional, fresher, and local foods, is conflated with authenticity and safety and opposed to the dangerous and porous present condition.

The Rules of the Game

Due to advancements in transportation, communication, and computing, today's globalization feels quicker and more intense to those who are affected by it. Media diffuse and amplify news from all corners of the world, twenty-four hours a day. Information is cheap and convenient, often accessible in the palms of our hands. Thanks to the financial instruments that allow fast, secure, and efficient movements of capital across borders, investors from the Persian Gulf can now buy land and invest in food production in Africa, Southeast Asia, and South America. New technologies provide easy access to real-time data, allowing operators to buy, stock, manage, and sell products, inputs, and financial instruments rapidly and efficiently. Investors in Tokyo can be updated instantly about the price of pork belly on the New York stock exchange, use electronic means of payment to buy and sell, and, if convenient, have the product quickly delivered anywhere in the world. Or they can just buy commodity futures, with no intention of ever dealing with any actual goods, instead looking only for fast profits through market speculation.

These technological advances have ushered unprecedented forms of financialization into the food commodity markets, along with the involvement of new actors: international investors, sovereign funds, as well as pension and hedge funds. However, as they're not directly connected to the production, distribution, and consumption of food, such organizations can operate with little concern for the fate of consumers. Whole populations, in fact, have been suffering from the sudden spikes in food prices caused by market instability and speculation. In the absence of international agreements on the management of the financial aspects of food markets, these phenomena are likely to happen again—and possibly more frequently.

Moreover, economic recessions, climate change, political disturbances, and trade wars are likely to impact the availability of food and its global circulation. For this reason, new actors have been acquiring large tracts of productive land, especially in Africa. Among them, we can list sovereign funds from countries that are not able to produce food; small and large countries that want to be sure they have enough sustenance for their citizens in case of emergencies; and private investors looking to profit from possible price spikes. In the phenomenon known as *land grabbing*, plots and estates are not necessarily expropriated; farmers may be lured by ready cash to sell their properties—often with the complicity of local authorities and national governments in need of investments, infrastructure, and support.

At times, legal ownership of land doesn't change hands, but farmers sign agreements to sell whole harvests at an agreed-upon price to large corporations, distributors, or retail organizations in industrialized countries, such as large supermarket chains that distribute produce under their own brands. However, when agreeing to work under *contract farming*, as this form of agriculture is known, farmers also agree that their products will be accepted only if they meet precise specifications and standards, ranging from safety to dates of delivery and even appearance. Vegetables that do not reflect the aesthetic expectations of shoppers in the Global North may be refused, causing huge financial losses for the farmers. In these situations, food is expected to reflect Western value categories directly in its place of production and doesn't even leave the exporting country if it isn't considered on par with the needs and preferences of faraway buyers and consumers. What happens if the preferences of affluent shoppers change? What would the consequences be for farmers who bet their futures on satisfying these shoppers' demands?

More importantly, besides meeting the voluntary standards of contract farming, food for export primarily needs to abide to the rules laid out in the SPS Agreement of the WTO, as well as other international food safety regulations, such as those in the *Codex Alimentarius* (see chapter 3). Although their stated goal is to protect the health of humans, animals, and plants, measures based on the SPS Agreement are used not infrequently in trade disputes, resulting in discrimination or disguised restrictions that in practice can stop the import of foreign foods. However, to apply these measures, a country needs to provide sufficient scientific evidence for their urgency. Although such standards have proved crucial in terms of securing food safety at the global level, they also constitute indirect barriers to trade for less-developed countries. In general, Global North governments tend to apply much stricter standards, and they have the financial, administrative, and logistic means to apply and enforce them. Even when producers and exporters in developing countries comply with the international standards, which are extremely intricate, frequently updated, and require a high degree of expertise to apply, their national authorities may not have the capacity to provide the necessary certifications of compliance, jeopardizing the chances of successful export.

The rules of the game lean in favor of developed countries, both in terms of international agreements among sovereign nations and in global dynamics that are controlled by nongovernmental entities, from banks and investment funds to technology companies and food-processing and retail transnational corporations. The consequences of this state of affairs became painfully clear in 2007, when the prices of major food commodities suddenly skyrocketed, creating a widespread panic among the poorest consumers around the world. This cautionary tale demonstrates the need for profound changes in the food system if we want it to keep it functioning in the future.

The 2007–2008 Global Food Crisis: An Isolated Incident?

Port-au-Prince in Haiti, Douala in Cameroon, Maputo in Mozambique, the outskirts of Dhaka in Bangladesh, Jakarta in Indonesia: Between the end of 2007 and the spring of 2008, these places, so different both culturally and geographically, shared the common experience of demonstrations and riots, caused by sudden increases in food prices and bringing daily life to a halt. In Haiti, food expenses ballooned between 50 and 100 percent, causing the prime minister to resign. Overall, between March 2007 and March 2008, the world price of corn surged by 31 percent, rice 74 percent, soybeans 87 percent, and wheat a whopping 130 percent.[7] Prices declined from the end of 2008, but spiked again in 2011. Although they eventually decreased again and the global panic subsided, the food commodities affected by the spike are now more expensive than they were in 2007. Moreover, the same mechanisms that created those emergencies are still in place, so the risk for new price spikes is still present.

The immediate causes were export restrictions implemented by major rice producing countries like Bangladesh, India, Vietnam, and later China. Various factors contributed to such decisions: the aftermath of cyclone Sidr that hit Bangladesh at the end of 2007; the fear that a cold winter season in southern China and northern Vietnam could negatively impact the rice harvest; and the increase in the price of wheat, linked to reduced harvests in the 2005 to 2006 season in grain-producing countries. In the United States, the Midwest had been hit by floods, while Australia had suffered from a drought. Export restrictions caused panic among importing countries, where local governments tried to replenish their stocks by locking prices for large quantities of rice. The sudden expansion in demand drove up prices globally, while importing countries such as Nigeria, Iran, Indonesia, and Ghana lowered or eliminated tariffs on rice imports to keep the local prices low. Some governments ended up buying more grain than necessary as the decrease in rice harvests did not materialize.

Several political and financial occurrences also contributed to the panic. In 2007, the US Federal Reserve began to lower interest rates to counteract the alarm in the subprime mortgage markets in the United States. Investors moved capital into currencies with higher interest rates, which caused the US dollar to lose value and commodity prices—often traded in dollars—to go up. Moreover, the low interest rates reduced the cost of storage, creating an incentive to stock commodities right when their prices were rising. As the real estate market collapsed and the crisis expanded to the banking sector, international financial actors looked for new forms of investments to diversify their portfolios. They found them in food commodities, which became a target for speculation on stock markets. These shifts of capitals lead to a greater instability and sudden spikes in prices. In the same period, the declining dollar and the demand for oil in fast-growing economies like India and China was leading to an increase in the prices of fossil fuels, which in turn made agricultural inputs (fertilizers, pesticides), energy, and transportation more expensive. In March 2008, the price of oil reached one hundred dollars a barrel and the demand for biofuels started expanding, putting pressure on land use and shifting production from human food and animal feed to crops for biofuels, especially corn.

Long-term dynamics amplified the impact of the crisis. The increased consumer purchasing power in emerging economies such as India and China is reflected in a shift of food demand away from traditional staples and toward higher-value foods, such as meat (poultry, in the case of India), milk, and dairy, which require increasing amounts of animal feed, putting pressure on food production for human consumption. More importantly, global agriculture, especially in developing countries, has been suffering since the 1980s from the consequences of the worldwide adoption of the economic framework known as the *Washington Consensus*. This approach to international relations favors the free circulation of capital and the deregulation of economic activities. These shifts entail the elimination of trade barriers among countries, the privatization of public assets, and the centrality of intellectual property rights in regulating markets and production. The Washington Consensus shaped the structural readjustment programs that the World Bank and the International Monetary Fund (IMF) imposed on developing countries in the 1980s in exchange for reducing the international debt incurred in previous years. The low interest rates of the early 1970s, supported by the abundance of capital from oil-producing countries, had led many governments to borrow heavily in an attempt to boost economic development. However, when Chairman Paul Volcker of the US Federal Reserve suddenly raised interest rates to rein in inflation in the United States in 1979, the cost of servicing their debt skyrocketed.

The first country to default on its debt was Mexico, in the early 1980s, followed by many others. The IMF agreed to finance the debt in exchange for structural adjustment reforms that privatized national enterprises and natural resources, exposing them to unregulated private speculation and opening countries to free trade and foreign direct investments. These reforms refocused whole sectors toward export-led activities and reduced the role of the public sector in agriculture through the elimination of subsidies and the marketing boards that oversaw maintaining price stability. The shock caused by these measures triggered a decline in long-term investment in agricultural research and development, extension, and rural infrastructures. The removal of agricultural tariffs led to a surge in imported crops from richer countries, which were cheaper than local products thanks to the subsidies that supported them. At the same time, the focus on export crops made the agricultural sector more vulnerable to the volatility of global prices, increasing many countries' dependence on food imports.

The new reality was reflected in the agreements that established the WTO in 2004. Among these, the most important for food was the Agreement on Agriculture, based on three pillars: insuring equal access to all members' markets through the progressive conversion of nontariff barriers (quotas, sanctions, embargoes) into tariffs; increasing international competition through the reduction of export subsidies and elimination of dumping; and transitioning internal agricultural support from subsidies, considered to cause price distortions on the international market, to direct payments and other forms of support that are not directly tied to agricultural yields and production. Although the Agreement on Agriculture included special and differential treatment for less-developed countries, at the time that the WTO agreements were negotiated, most Global

South countries were reeling from the economic shocks caused by structural adjustment measures and were not in a strong position to impose demands. Negotiations within the WTO are under way, and developing countries are joining efforts to be more effective in getting favorable terms. The results will determine the future direction of the global food system, which also is being affected by the threats of trade wars from new populist and nationalist governments in several Global North countries.

New Perspectives

The new world order of free trade has enormously increased the level of interconnection within the global food system. Although millions of individuals and communities still survive on subsistence agriculture, they can't avoid the consequences of mechanisms that, as removed from them as they may seem, deeply influence their production decisions, their business opportunities, their choices as consumers, and their standards of living.

Philanthropic organizations such as the Bill & Melinda Gates Foundation and Rockefeller Foundation, as well as governments, corporations, financial institutions, and NGOs, tend to look at solutions that are meant to improve existing structures and dynamics without questioning their validity and legitimacy. Besides favoring the intensification of production, interventions often focus on increased market integration and efficiency, better risk management, and increased control and transparency in the financial market. They also support public-private partnerships, promoting social responsibility on the part of corporations. Other schemes, such as fair trade, microfinance of projects for women or minorities, and various forms of development aid, have been launched to help farmers, especially in the least developed countries. Slow Food, an association founded in Italy at the end of the 1980s and now present all over the world, strives for "clean, fair, and good" food. A budding and still uncoordinated food movement is growing in many countries, focusing on diverse issues and at times representing contradictory interests. These are important steps, but much still needs to be done to make our global food system fairer, more sustainable, and more diverse.

Rather than looking for improvements, some grassroots organizations and social movements have proposed radically alternative approaches that question the basic principles of the existing food system. Such perspectives are meant to usher an equitable global food system and participative governance regimes. Consumer cooperatives establish direct connections with producers and distributors, creating different forms of shopping and participating in the shared goals of all those involved. Localized and embedded within rural communities around the world (including in the Global North), *La Via Campesina* ("the farmers' way," in Spanish) is among the most vocal actors in critiquing the power relations that determine the well-being, the economic outlook, and even the health of rural populations around the world.[8] Officially launched in 1993, La Via Campesina is a self-governing and diverse movement that coordinates grassroots peasant organizations and does not include NGOs, foundations, institutions, or aid agencies. Promoting an internationalism that aims at reconstructing and reviving a shared peasant identity, the movement doesn't shy away from combative attitudes, demonstrations, and antagonistic discussions. La Via Campesina became visible with the 1999 protests against the WTO, pushing for agrarian reforms and highlighting the damage inflicted on rural communities by unbridled free trade. A less confrontational approach is proposed by *Terra Madre*, the biannual meeting of farmers organized by Slow Food during its *Salone del Gusto*, a meeting of producers and consumers of traditional and artisanal foods. At Terra Madre, participants share experiences and work together to identify common positions and action propositions, but without the political assertiveness of La Via Campesina.

The perspective these movements embrace is referred to as *food sovereignty*, which refers to the right of communities at all scales, from a village to a whole nation, to democratic self-determination about what food is grown, imported, distributed, and eaten. It is a form of resistance to the dominant role that transnational food corporations, international organizations, banks and other financial institutions have played in shaping the food system. According to the Declaration of Nyéléni, approved in 2007 by delegates from eighty countries at the Forum for Food Sovereignty in Sélingué, Mali:

> Food sovereignty is the right of peoples to healthy and culturally appropriate food produced through ecologically sound and sustainable methods, and their right to define their own food and agriculture systems. It puts the aspirations and needs of those who produce, distribute and consume food at the heart of food systems and policies rather than the demands of markets and corporations. It defends the interests and inclusion of the next generation. It offers a strategy to resist and dismantle the current corporate trade and food regime, and directions for food, farming, pastoral and fisheries systems determined by local producers and users. Food sovereignty prioritises local and national economies and markets and empowers peasant and family farmer-driven agriculture, artisanal fishing, pastoralist-led grazing, and food production, distribution and consumption based on environmental, social and economic sustainability.

Food sovereignty ... refers to the right of communities at all scales, from a village to a whole nation, to democratic self-determination about what food is grown, imported, distributed, and eaten.

Food sovereignty promotes transparent trade that guarantees just incomes to all peoples as well as the rights of consumers to control their food and nutrition. It ensures that the rights to use and manage lands, territories, waters, seeds, livestock and biodiversity are in the hands of those of us who produce food. Food sovereignty implies new social relations free of oppression and inequality between men and women, peoples, racial groups, social and economic classes and generations.[9]

Just as business, finance, and trade operate globally, so too do resistance movements, generating networks and transnational connections among diverse organizations and groups that embrace positions ranging from reform and improvement of the current food system to radical critiques and calls to dismantle it. Food sovereignty is one of the more successful approaches for mobilizing producers and consumers, especially in the Global South. Of course, other approaches also aim to change the current situation, from food and environmental justice to local activism, antihunger efforts, urban farming, food hubs, farmers' markets, and community-supported agriculture.

What are we to do as consumers, when it seems impossible for us to have any influence on the complex dynamics that determine what is available to eat? While large segments of citizens in postindustrial societies still struggle to put food on their tables, some among those who have wider choices express their dissatisfaction with the present state of things by opting for locavorism, trying to limit their consumption to food grown and produced nearby by people they are familiar with. Some join community gardens, cooperatives, community-supported agriculture initiatives, and direct forms of participation. Some choose engagement and advocacy within the wide spectrum of the food movement, with the goal of social and political change. Some prefer to focus on food as a form of cultural expression and aesthetic experience, honing their expertise on topics ranging from ethnic cuisines to wine. These perspectives are not mutually exclusive: consumers may embrace several, fully or in part, depending on their personal and communal context.

It has become increasingly clear that real and profound change in the global food system can be generated only by collective political action leading to systemic changes. Food should become a central topic in the political platforms of candidates running for office at the local and national levels. Voters should put pressure on legislators and governments to pass laws and adopt policies that not only reflect the interests of the food industry or limited constituencies, but also prioritize the well-being of all citizens, including the most vulnerable ones. Global issues like the environment, sustainability, climate change, migration, finance, trade, and technology should be addressed at the international level. It isn't enough for large companies that ultimately gain from this state of things to green-wash their operations or to invest resources into social responsibility projects when those same funds—which would increase if profit were not the only priority—could be invested for real change and to better the lives of their employees, as a start.[10] Transnational social movements, NGOs, and civil societies are increasingly involved in negotiations that lead to global conventions and resolutions. It may be not enough, but it's a start. We need to remind ourselves that we are not just consumers, but citizens. Determining what the future will look like is our collective responsibility. It's not enough to vote with our wallets.

GLOSSARY

Agrobiodiversity
The diversity of agricultural and animal species resulting from natural selection operated by farmers, shepherds, and fishermen over centuries.

Appertization
A process named after its inventor, the French confectioner Nicholas Appert. It destroys microorganisms in food through exposure to very high temperatures, usually by sealing the food in airtight containers and placing them in boiling water.

Biofuels
Fuels produced from organic matter through various industrialized biological processes that take place rapidly rather than over millennia, as in the case of fossil fuels. Biofuels include *bioethanol*, made through fermentation from sugar or starch crops; and *biodiesel*, made from vegetable oils and animal fats. Second-generation biofuels are produced from nonfood cellulosic biomasses like agricultural waste and woody crops, whereas third-generation ones are based on algae, fungi, and other microorganisms.

Blockchain
Technology that allows all the participants in a network to have access to a dispersed database of transactions (known as a *digital ledger*) and provide independent confirmation for them.

Community-supported agriculture (CSA)
An agricultural supply network in which consumers agree with farmers in advance to buy their harvest or a portion of it, usually delivered at agreed-upon intervals.

Contract farming
Agricultural production based on a written arrangement between buyers (usually large corporations, distributors, or retail organizations) and farmers, who maintain the ownership of their land but agree to sell a specific crop at an agreed-upon price, so long as the product meets specifications and standards imposed by the buyers, ranging from safety standards to dates of delivery and even the appearance of the produce.

Externalities
Expected or unexpected side effects of a productive activity that impacts other parties but the cost of which is not factored into the final cost of the goods or services derived from that activity. Externalities can be *positive*, as in the landscape management often connected with agricultural activities, or *negative*, like the release of sluices from animal farms into public waters, which then require purification at the taxpayers' expense.

Financialization of food commodities
Massive investments and speculation on commodities in stock markets from actors that are not directly involved in the production, distribution, and consumption of food (international investors, sovereign funds, and pension and hedge funds).

Foodshed
Conceptually analogous to a watershed, this term indicates the geographic area from which food flows toward a specific location and its population (producers, distributors, and consumers).

Foodways
The practices connected to the production, processing, distribution, preparation, and consumption of food in a given community.

Food desert
An area where fresh and nutritious food is not available, with a prevalence instead of outlets selling fast food or highly processed, prepackaged products.

Food fad
A short-lived food-related practice that captures the imagination of consumers through media and celebrities.

Food miles
The distance between the production site of food and its end destination. This statistic is mostly used to measure the consumption of fossil fuels and other forms of energy necessary for transportation.

Food movement
Various political, social, and cultural initiatives the goal of which is to bring change to the food system, which is perceived as deficient and in crisis. Although they are unrelated, such initiatives are often perceived as expressions of a large, albeit unorganized, social movement.

Food regime
An analytical approach established in the 1980s by Harriet Friedmann and Philip McMichael to define ways of organizing a food system that reflect production structures and power relations among its actors.

Food safety
Prevention of food-borne illnesses. Food-safety measures extend to the production, processing, distribution, storage, preparation, and consumption of food.

Food security
According to the definition adopted in 1996 at the World Food Summit by the Food and Agriculture Organization of the United Nations (FAO), "Food security exists when all people, at all times, have physical and economic access to sufficient, safe and nutritious food to meet their dietary needs and food preferences for an active and healthy life. The four pillars of food security are availability, stability of supply, access and utilization."

Food sovereignty
The right of communities at all scales, from a village to a whole nation, to democratic self-determination regarding what food is grown, distributed, imported, and eaten.

Food system
The totality of structures, infrastructures, dynamics, processes, networks, and relations that determine the production, manufacturing, distribution, marketing, sales, consumption, and disposal of food.

Global North
A general term used to indicate the most economically developed countries, such as Canada, the United States, Western Europe, and Japan, located in the Northern Hemisphere, together with Australia and New Zealand in the Southern Hemisphere.

Global South
A general term that refers to countries that have not reached the level of development that characterizes the Global North, including superpowers such as Russia, China, and India, as well as other nations in Central and South America, Africa, the Middle East, South Asia, and Southeast Asia.

Genetically modified organism (GMO)
An organism whose genes have been transferred from varieties in the same species or from other species.

Green revolution
A new approach to agriculture, promoted from the late 1960s, that aimed to increase agricultural output by introducing new high-yield crop varieties, often with the support of fertilizers, pesticides, irrigation, and mechanization.

Hunger
The physical and psychological consequences of lack of food, often mediated by cultural perception and social dynamics.

Internet of Things (IoT)
The connections among everyday devices (tools, machineries, sensors, software, and mobile applications) and human users to exchange data and information through the internet.

Land grabbing
Acquisition of large tracts of private or public land by national or transnational actors, often with the mediation of local authorities and national governments.

Locavorism
The choice of limiting acquisition and consumption of food to items grown and produced as close as possible to the point of consumption.

Monoculture
The practice of growing a single crop at a time in a farm or on a field. Often practiced in extensive and mechanized agriculture.

Nutrient
A substance that living organisms need to grow and survive.

Nutrition
The word refers to both the necessary amount and variety of food and water required by living organisms to survive and the processes through which such substances are metabolized.

Nutritional label
A label required in most countries on prepackaged foods, carrying nutritional information considered relevant for consumers.

Nutritionism
Excessive or exclusive focus on individual nutrients, taken out of the food context in which they are found, in order to maximize their supposed impact on specific aspects of physiology and health.

Organic agriculture
A production system that avoids the excessive use of industrially produced chemical inputs, emphasizing the health of soils, the ecological systems and processes that best support it, biodiversity, and farming communities.

Supply chain
The linear sequence of processes, actors, and locations involved in the production, distribution, and sale of a commodity, from start to end.

Supply network
The complex network that connects multiple nodes directly and indirectly involved in the production, distribution, and sale of a commodity. It differs from a supply chain in that it expands a linear process to include all the factors that may impact it, extending it to external nodes and multidirectional connections.

Sustainability
Socioecological processes that look at maintaining the long-term functionality and productivity of a system in terms of its environmental impact, its social fairness, and its economic viability.

Taste

This refers to both the flavor and organoleptic attributes of a food (as in, "this food tastes good") and the capacity to judge its value and appropriateness (as in, "this meal is in good taste").

Traceability

The ability to trace a product through all stages of production, processing, distribution, and retail while identifying the actors involved at each stage, generally through the use of technology such as barcodes and blockchain.

NOTES

1 Food: A Citizen's Manual

1. Although descriptors such as Global North/Global South and developed/ underdeveloped/developing countries risk erasing distinctions among countries and can hide important dynamics internal to individual countries, such as class or ethnicity, they allow for introducing crucial general concepts that will be discussed in further detail when necessary.

2. See https://www.bergamonews.it/2011/05/13/s-alla-polenta-no-al-cous -cousla-lega-ne-distribuisce-800-chili/145882/.

3. See https://www.politico.eu/article/a-polish-game-of-tapes/.

4. S. Margot Finn, *Discriminating Taste: How Class Anxiety Created the American Food Revolution* (New Brunswick, NJ: Rutgers University Press, 2017).

5. See https://www.danchurchaid.org/where-we-work/palestine/promotion -of-urban-gardening-in-gaza.

6. See http://www.ipsnews.net/2008/12/south-africa-community-gardens -contribute-to-food-security/.

7. See https://www.dissapore.com/primo-piano/con-i-panini-mcitaly-vivace-e -adagio-oltre-a-minuetto-gualtiero-marchesi-puo-stringere-la-mano-al -collega-ronald-mcdonalds/.

8. See https://www.rollingstone.com/music/music-news/burger-king-pulls -controversial-mary-j-blige-ad-103625/.

9. Laura Lindenfeld and Fabio Parasecoli, *Feasting Our Eyes: Food Films and Cultural Identity in the United States* (New York: Columbia University Press, 2016).

2 Making Sense of Food Systems

1. Fabio Parasecoli, *Knowing Where It Comes From: Labeling Traditional Foods to Compete in a Global Market* (Iowa City: University of Iowa Press, 2017).

2. Peter J. Atkins, Peter Lummel, and Derek J. Oddy, *Food and the City in Europe since 1800* (Burlington, VT: Ashgate, 2007).

3. Susanne Freidberg, *Fresh: A Perishable History* (Cambridge, MA: Harvard University Press, 2010).

4. Harriet Friedman and Philip McMichael, "Agriculture and the State System: The Rise and Decline of National Agricultures, 1870 to the Present," *Sociologia Ruralis* 29, no. 2 (1989): 93–117.

5. Raj Patel, *Stuffed and Starved: The Hidden Battle for the World Food System* (New York: Melville House Publishing, 2007), 12.

6. See https://www.ers.usda.gov/amber-waves/2014/april/china-in-the-next -decade-rising-meat-demand-and-growing-imports-of-feed/.

7. See https://www.ers.usda.gov/webdocs/publications/82639/ldpm-272-01 .pdf?v=42800.

8. See https://www.weforum.org/agenda/2016/12/this-map-shows-how-much -each-country-spends-on-food/.

9. See https://www.ers.usda.gov/data-products/chart-gallery/gallery/chart -detail/?chartId=58372.

10. William Bertrand and Elke de Buhr, "Trade, Development and Child Labor: Regulation and Law in the Case of Child Labor in the Cocoa Industry," *Law and Development Review* 8, no. 2 (2015): 503–521.

11. See https://data.worldbank.org/indicator/SP.URB.TOTL.IN.ZS.

12. See https://data.worldbank.org/indicator/SP.RUR.TOTL.ZS.

13. Branden Born and Mark Purcell, "Avoiding the Local Trap: Scale and Food Systems in Planning Research," *Journal of Planning Education and Research* 26, no. 2 (2006): 195–207.

3 Health and Nutrition

1. The US Burden of Disease Collaborators, "The State of US Health, 1990–2016.

Burden of Diseases, Injuries, and Risk Factors among US States," *Journal of the American Medical Association* 319, no. 14 (2018):1444–1472.

2. An exhaustive database of policies aimed at promoting healthy diets is provided by the World Cancer Research Fund International through the NOURISHING framework, available at https://www.wcrf.org/int/policy/ nourishing-database.

3. Global data about obesity is available at http://www.who.int/gho/ncd/ risk_factors/overweight/en/.

4. See https://www.who.int/en/news-room/fact-sheets/detail/obesity-and -overweight.

5. Marion Nestle, *Food Politics: How the Food Industry Influences Nutrition and Health* (Berkeley: University of California Press, 2013).

6. Marion Nestle, *Unsavory Truth: How Food Companies Skew the Science of What We Eat* (New York: Basic Books, 2018).

7. Marion Nestle, "Food Industry Funding of Nutrition Research: The Relevance of History for Current Debates," *JAMA Internal Medicine* 176, no. 11 (2016):1685–1686.

8. Gyorgy Scrinis, *Nutritionism: The Science and Politics of Dietary Advice* (New York: Columbia University Press, 2013), 2.

9. See http://www.minsal.cl/ley-de-alimentos-nuevo-etiquetado-de-alimentos.

10. See https://ec.europa.eu/food/safety/labelling_nutrition/labelling_legis lation_en.

11. Joseph C. Hannon et al., "Advances and Challenges for the Use of Engineered Nanoparticles in Food Contact Materials," *Trends in Food Science & Technology* 43, no. 1 (2015): 43–62.

12. See https://www.nhs.uk/news/food-and-diet/new-colour-coded-food-nu trition-labels-launched/.

13. See https://www.santepubliquefrance.fr/Sante-publique-France/Nutri -Score.

14. See https://www.fda.gov/Food/GuidanceRegulation/GuidanceDocuments RegulatoryInformation/LabelingNutrition/ucm385663.htm.

15. The seven food groups were leafy greens and yellow vegetables; citrus fruits, tomatoes, and raw cabbage; potatoes and other vegetables and fruits; dairy; proteins, including pulses; cereals and derived products; and butter and margarine.

16. See https://www.cnpp.usda.gov/FGP.

17. For India's model, see http://ninindia.org/DietaryGuidelinesforNINweb site.pdf; for China's, see http://www.fao.org/nutrition/education/food-dietary -guidelines/regions/countries/china/en/.

18. See https://www.cnpp.usda.gov/mypyramid.

19. See https://www.choosemyplate.gov/MyPlate.

20. See https://www.gov.uk/government/publications/the-eatwell-guide.

21. See http://www.mhlw.go.jp/bunya/kenkou/pdf/eiyou-syokuji5.pdf.

22. See http://www.fao.org/3/a-as866s.pdf.

23. Zofia Boni, "Contested Interactions: School Shops, Children and Food in Warsaw," *International Journal of Sociology of Agriculture & Food* 21, no. 3 (2014): 309–325.

24. See http://www.fnde.gov.br/programas/pnae.

25. See http://www.siteal.iipe.unesco.org/politica/999/alimentacion-comple mentaria-escolar-ace.

26. See http://eduscol.education.fr/cid47664/l-importance-d-une-education -nutritionnelle.html.

27. See http://www.legout.com/la-semaine-du-gout/.

28. See http://www.maff.go.jp/e/pdf/shokuiku.pdf.

29. See https://www.slowfood.com/edible-school-gardens/.

30. See https://edibleschoolyard.org/.

31. See http://www.jamiesfoodrevolution.org/ for more information.

32. See http://www.fao.org/fao-who-codexalimentarius/en/.

4 Environment and Sustainability

1. Mark F. Bellemare et al., "On the Measurement of Food Waste," *American Journal of Agricultural Economics* 99, no. 5 (2017): 1148–1158.

2. FAO, *Food Wastage Footprint: Impacts on Natural Resources* (Rome: FAO, 2013), http://www.fao.org/docrep/018/i3347e/i3347e.pdf.

3. Conrad Zach et al., "Relationship between Food Waste, Diet Quality, and Environmental Sustainability," *PLoS ONE* 13, no. 4 (2018): e0195405, https://doi.org/10.1371/journal.pone.0195405.

4. Paul Johnston et al., "Reclaiming the Definition of Sustainability," *Environmental Science & Pollution Research* 14, no.1 (2007): 60–66.

5. More information is available at http://www.noaa.gov/media-release/gulf-of-mexico-dead-zone-is-largest-ever-measured.

6. Jill Lindsay Harrison, *Pesticide Drift and the Pursuit of Environmental Justice* (Cambridge, MA: MIT Press, 2011).

7. Elinor Ostrom, *Governing the Commons: The Evolution of Institutions for Collective Action* (Cambridge: Cambridge University Press, 1990).

8. L. H. Dietterich et al., "Impacts of Elevated Atmospheric CO_2 on Nutrient Content of Important Food Crops," *Nature Scientific Data* 2 (2015): 150036, https://doi.org/10.1038/sdata.2015.36.

9. Data available at http://www.worldometers.info/water/.

10. Kyle Frankel Davis, "Increased Food Production and Reduced Water Use through Optimized Crop Distribution," *Nature Geoscience* 10 (2017): 919–924.

11. Karthik Balaguru, Gregory R. Foltz, and L. Ruby Leung, "Increasing Magnitude of Hurricane Rapid Intensification in the Central and Eastern Tropical Atlantic," *Geophysical Research Letters* 45, no. 9 (2018): 4238–4247; Ehsan Najafi et al., "Understanding the Changes in Global Crop Yields through Changes in Climate and Technology," *Earth's Future* 6, no. 3 (2018): 410–427.

5 Technology

1. Warren Belasco, *Meals to Come: A History of the Future of Food* (Berkeley: University of California Press, 2006).

2. Maxime Bilet and Nathan Myhrvold, *Modernist Cuisine: The Art and Science of Cooking* (Bellevue, WA: Cooking Lab, 2011).

3. Hervé This, *Molecular Gastronomy: Exploring the Science of Flavor* (New York: Columbia University Press, 2008).

4. Rachel Laudan, "A Plea for Culinary Modernism: Why We Should Love New, Fast, Processed Food." *Gastronomica* 1, no. 1 (2001): 36–44.

5. John H. Perkins, *Geopolitics and the Green Revolution: Wheat, Genes, and the Cold War* (New York: Oxford University Press, 1997).

6. Two opposite evaluations of the green revolution can be found in Vandana Shiva, *The Violence of the Green Revolution: Third World Agriculture, Ecology, and Politics* (London: Zed Books, 1991); and Gordon Convay, *The Doubly Green Revolution: Food for All in the Twenty-first Century* (Ithaca, NY: Cornell University Press, 1998).

7. See http://www.fao.org/docrep/003/x9602e/x9602e06.htm.

8. Sakiko Fukuda-Parr, ed., *The Gene Revolution: GM Crops and Unequal Development* (Sterling, VA: Earthscan, 2007).

9. See https://www.cbc.ca/news/canada/biotech-giant-wins-supreme-court-battle-1.474200.

10. Ronald J. Herring, "Stealth Seeds: Bioproperty, Biosafety, Biopolitics," *Journal of Peasant Studies* 36, no. 1 (2009): 130–157.

11. See https://aerofarms.com/.

12. See https://www.straitstimes.com/lifestyle/home-design/fresh-ideas-for-city-farms.

13. See https://www.beckersasc.com/gastroenterology-and-endoscopy/harvard-gastroenterologist-partners-with-artist-on-qmouth-to-anusq-camera-pill-project.html.

14. Joshua Lederberg and Alexa T. McCray, "Ome Sweet 'Omics: A Genealogical Treasury of Words," *The Scientist* 15, no. 7 (2001): 8, http://www. the-scientist.com/?articles.view/articleNo/13313/title/-Ome-Sweet--Omics-A-Genealogical-Treasury-of-Words/.

15. See https://www.impossiblefoods.com/.

16. See http://www.fdna.org/#FoundingDoc.

6 Hunger and Food Security

1. See http://www.fao.org/3/a-y7937e.pdf.

2. Ancel Keys et al., *The Biology of Human Starvation* (Minneapolis: University of Minnesota Press, 1950).

3. James Donnelly Jr., *The Great Irish Potato Famine* (Stroud, UK: History Press, 2008).

4. Mike Davis, *Late Victorian Holocausts: El Niño Famines and the Making of the Third World* (New York: Verso, 2000).

5. Charles Roland, *Courage Under Siege: Disease, Starvation and Death in the Warsaw Ghetto* (New York: Oxford University Press, 1992); Michael and

Elizabeth Norman, *Tears in the Darkness: The Story of the Bataan Death March and Its Aftermath* (New York: Picador, 2010).

6. See https://www.un.org/sustainabledevelopment/sustainable-development-goals/.

7. See http://www.fao.org/state-of-food-security-nutrition/en/.

8. United Nations Human Rights and FAO, *The Right to Adequate Food* (New York: United Nations, 2010), http://www.ohchr.org/Documents/Publications/FactSheet34en.pdf.

9. See http://foodsecurityindex.eiu.com/.

10. Martin Bruegel, ed., *Profusion et Pénurie: Les Hommes Face à Leur Besoins Alimentaires* (Tours, France: Presses universitaires François-Rabelais, 2009), 14–15; translation mine.

11. Janet Poppendieck, *Sweet Charity: Emergency Food and the End of Entitlement* (New York: Penguin Books, 1999).

12. Andrew Fisher, *Big Hunger: The Unholy Alliance between Corporate America and Anti-Hunger Groups* (Cambridge, MA: MIT Press, 2017).

13. Erica Kohl-Arena, *The Self-Help Myth: How Philanthropy Fails to Alleviate Poverty* (Berkeley: California University Press, 2015).

14. Amartya Sen, *Poverty and Famines: An Essay on Entitlement and Deprivation* (Oxford: Oxford University Press, 1990), 154–155.

15. See http://www.srfood.org/images/stories/pdf/officialreports/20140310_finalreport_en.pdf.

16. Pete Daniel, *Dispossession: Discrimination against African American Farmers in the Age of Civil Rights* (Chapel Hill: University of North Carolina Press, 2013).

17. See https://www.ers.usda.gov/topics/food-nutrition-assistance/food-security-in-the-us/.

18. See https://www.gsb.stanford.edu/faculty-research/working-papers/geography-poverty-nutrition-food-deserts-food-choices-across-united.

19. See http://www.climatecentre.org/.

7 What Happens Next?

1. Kathleen Lebesco and Peter Naccarato, *Culinary Capital* (Oxford: Berg, 2012).

2. Hasia Diner, *Hungering for America: Italian, Irish, and Jewish Foodways in the Age of Migration* (Cambridge, MA: Harvard University Press, 2001); Donna Gabaccia, *We Are What We Eat: Ethnic Food and the Making of Americans* (Cambridge, MA: Harvard University Press, 1998).

3. Krishnendu Ray, *The Ethnic Restaurateur* (New York: Bloomsbury, 2016).

4. Fabio Parasecoli, *Knowing Where It Comes From: Labeling Traditional Foods to Compete in a Global Market* (Iowa City: University of Iowa Press, 2017), 181–202.

5. Alfred Crosby, *Ecological Imperialism: The Biological Expansion of Europe, 900–1900*, 2nd ed. (New York: Cambridge University Press, 2004).

6. Claude Fischler, *L'Homnivore: Le goût, la cuisine et le corps* (Paris: Odile Jacob, 1990).

7. See http://news.bbc.co.uk/1/hi/world/7284196.stm.

8. See https://viacampesina.org/en/.

9. See https://nyeleni.org/spip.php?article290.

10. Anand Giridharadas, *Winners Take All: The Elite Charade of Changing the World* (New York: Alfred A. Knopf, 2018).

FURTHER READING

Barber, Dan. *The Third Plate: Field Notes on the Future of Food*. New York: Penguin, 2014.

Caparrós, Martín. *Hunger: The Mortal Crisis of Our Time*. New York: Other Press, 2017.

Choi, Jaz Hee-jong, Marcus Foth, and Greg Hearn, ed. *Eat, Cook, Grow: Mixing Human-Computer Interactions with Human-Food Interactions*. Cambridge, MA: MIT Press, 2014.

Clapp, Jennifer. *Food*. Malden, MA: Polity Press, 2012.

Cornon, William. *Nature's Metropolis: Chicago and the Great West*. New York: W. W. Norton & Company, 1991.

Federico, Giovanni. *Feeding the World: An Economic History of Agriculture, 1800–2000*. Princeton, NJ: Princeton University Press, 2005.

Ferrières, Madeleine. *Sacred Cow, Mad Cow: A History of Food Fears*. New York: Columbia University Press, 2006.

Greenberg, Paul. *Four Fish: The Future of the Last Wild Food*. New York: Penguin Books, 2010.

Guthman, Julie. *Weighing In: Obesity, Food Justice, and the Limits of Capitalism*. Berkeley: University of California Press, 2011.

Harvey, David. *A Brief History of Neoliberalism*. New York: Oxford University Press, 2005.

Hesterman, Oran. *Fair Food: Growing a Healthy, Sustainable Food System for All*. New York: PublicAffairs, 2011.

Horwitz, Jamie, and Paulette Singley, ed. *Eating Architecture*. Cambridge, MA: MIT Press, 2004.

Levenstein, Harvey. *Fear of Food: A History of Why We Worry about What We Eat*. Chicago: University of Chicago Press, 2012.

McWilliams, James. *Eating Promiscuously: Adventures in the Future of Food*. Berkeley, CA: Counterpoint Press, 2017.

Nestle, Marion. *What to Eat*. New York: Farrar, Straus and Giroux, 2006.

Newman, Cara. *The Secret Financial Life of Food: From Commodities Markets to Supermarkets*. New York: Columbia University Press, 2013.

Paarlberg, Robert. *Food Politics: What Everyone Needs to Know*. New York: Oxford University Press, 2013.

Pollan. Michael. *In Defense of Food: An Eater's Manifesto*. New York: Penguin Books, 2008.

Roberts, Paul. *The End of Food*. New York: Mariner Books, 2008.

Schonwald, Josh. *The Taste of Tomorrow: Dispatches from the Future of Food*. New York: HarperCollins, 2012.

Spencer, Colin. *The Heretic's Feast: A History of Vegetarianism*. Hanover, NH: University Press of New England, 1995.

Vernon, James. *Hunger: A Modern History*. Cambridge, MA: Belknap Press of Harvard University Press, 2007.

Vodeb, Oliver, ed. *Food Democracy: Critical Lessons in Food, Communication, Design and Art*. Bristol, UK: Intellect, 2017.

Westhoff, Patrick. *The Economics of Food: How Feeding and Fueling the Planet Affects Food Prices*. Upper Saddle River, NJ: Pearson Education, 2010.

INDEX

The MIT Press Essential Knowledge Series

FABIO PARASECOLI is a professor in the Department of Nutrition and Food Studies at New York University. Previously, he was a professor and the director of food studies initiatives at the New School in New York City, where he launched the AA and BA/BS degrees in food studies. He wrote for many years as the US correspondent for *Gambero Rosso*, Italy's authoritative food and wine magazine. Recent books include *Bite Me: Food in Popular Culture* (2008), the six-volume *A Cultural History of Food* (2012; coedited with Peter Scholliers), *Al Dente: A History of Food in Italy* (2014; translated into Italian in 2015 and into Korean in 2018), *Feasting Our Eyes: Food Films and Cultural Identity in the United States* (2016; with Laura Lindenfeld), and *Knowing Where It Comes From: Labeling Traditional Foods to Compete in a Global Market* (2017).